From Geordie Land to No Mans Land

George Russell Elder

AuthorHouse™
1663 Liberty Drive
Bloomington, IN 47403
www.authorhouse.com
Phone: 1-800-839-8640

First published by AuthorHouse 9/14/2011

ISBN: 978-1-4520-0651-2 (sc)
ISBN: 978-1-4520-0652-9 (hc)
ISBN: 978-1-4567-8868-1 (e)

Printed in the United States of America

This book is printed on acid-free paper.

George Russell Elder dedicates this book to his pal **Edward Watmough** who died in action on 31st August 1918 whilst George was on home leave.

This book is taken from 6 diaries written by George Russell Elder shortly after the First World War. In his lifetime George made several unsuccessful attempts to have his diaries published but due to a lack of funds and his inability to find a sponsor the diaries remained unpublished until now. Before he died in 1980 he left these diaries with his daughter Mabel Chapelhow. Upon her death in 1993 the diaries passed to her children.

Without the cumulative efforts from the people below these captivating diaries would never have reached publication:-

Steven Chapelhow and Maureen Temple where the diaries were cherished and well looked after until 2008, when the family decided it was time to get them published.

Lynn Wakefield, *Granddaughter to George*, Lynn together with her husband Peter spent numerous hours deciphering the hand written notes and typing them up into a readable format.

Vivienne Toon, *Granddaughter to George*, Vivienne researched many aspects of the book and the family tree to add some context to the stories and post war days of George. Vivienne and her husband John fully financed the publishing of these diaries, and John has contributed many hours to researching; co-editing the book and formatting the final drafts for print.

Claire Thomas, *Great Granddaughter to George*, Claire also assisted with the co-editing of the book and together with her husband Paul, a serving musician in Her Majesty's Coldstream Guards suggested contacting the Army's Benevolent Fund for advice on the diaries. This resulted in several meetings with their CEO, Major General Sir Evelyn Webb Carter KCVO, OBE, DL, who kindly agreed to validate the diaries against war records and supply some historical context and images to many sections of George's accounts.

We would like to extend a very special thanks to Major General Sir Evelyn Webb Carter KCVO, OBE, DL, for his invaluable contribution to the publication of this book, and to all the family members mentioned above for their hard work and tenacity, without which we would never have made it. Finally a thank you to the Father, Grandfather, and Great Grandfather, George Russell Elder for sharing with us his memoirs

"Geordie Land to No Man's Land".

Front cover photos:- 18 pounder gun & George Russell Elder

Back cover photo:- George & Mildred Elder in 1970

CONTENTS

24 April 2011

FOREWORD

by

Major General Sir Evelyn Webb-Carter KCVO, OBE, DL

This story is about George Elder who in 1915 like millions of others as a young man left his secure employment and family in Newcastle to join the Territorial Force and go to France. He was not sure why he should volunteer but his instinct was strong that he should somehow serve his Nation and King. These old fashioned values are hard to comprehend today but they were strong and produced an Army of several million. Today the King's Troop Royal Horse Artillery fire blank rounds from their 13 pounder guns as a salute on Royal or State occasions. That gun came into service at the same time as the 18 pounder which George Elder spent his four year working with. So the links with the First World War are not that distant and relations still recall through diaries and family legend the sacrifice made in those terrible years of conflict.

I was shown these diaries a year ago and immediately recognised their value as a unique and well written record of the life of a gunner. George Elder neatly wrote his account in five exercise books between May 6th 1927 and June 1929. His script is precise and clear and it is quite probable that this labour of love was in response to the tragic events which his family at the time were experiencing. He wrote with the help of notes he made during the war and which was in itself an illegal act, as diaries were not permitted under strict security regulations. Collectively, George's family were enlisted to edit them and have done an excellent job in turning a great deal of prose into digestible chapters from which we as readers may discover the life as it really was in the Great War. I was approached as Chief Executive of the ABF, the Soldiers' Charity for advice but was fascinated by the story told in these pages. Having a rudimentary knowledge of the history of this period I volunteered to put a bit of context into the diaries. I have much enjoyed doing so and in the process have come to know in a rather curious way George Elder. Although no saint he was a great character and got himself into the odd jam but his accounts of life as a signaller in a Field Artillery Battery are most interesting. George was an observant man and his memory of events some twelve years later is remarkable. Occasionally his editors have found it difficult to cross reference his dates and this editor has from time to time made some alterations as to the order of events. The result is a pleasing and articulate account from the front line.

George was deeply affected by the death of his mate Ted Watmough who was killed in 1918 whilst George was on leave. They both came from Newcastle and George knew Ted's mother. The fact that his death occurred whilst George was away preyed on his mind and I expect was never far from his mind as he wrote his account of his four years and it is to Ted after all that these memoirs are dedicated.

Descriptions of his time in support of the infantry, in Base Hospital and during the riots in Harfleur are particularly well written and give a real flavour of what it was like for someone of Georges rank and standing. I was deeply saddened by the struggle that is evident in the postscript. George had done his duty with great distinction but his return to civilian life is marked with personal tragedy and hardship. All those who returned were supposed to enjoy a "country fit for heroes" but the reality, as is so often the case was very different and it is humbling to read of those difficult years of the 20s and 30s. The later generations have fared better and so it is fitting that his family led by his great granddaughter Claire Thomas who just remembers George should join together and publish his memoirs. Writing these would have caused him much reflection and pain but he would be pleased to see the result I am sure. I just hope he wouldn't have objected to some of my editing.

Evelyn Webb-Carter

FIRST WORLD WAR BATTLE SITES MENTIONED IN THIS BOOK

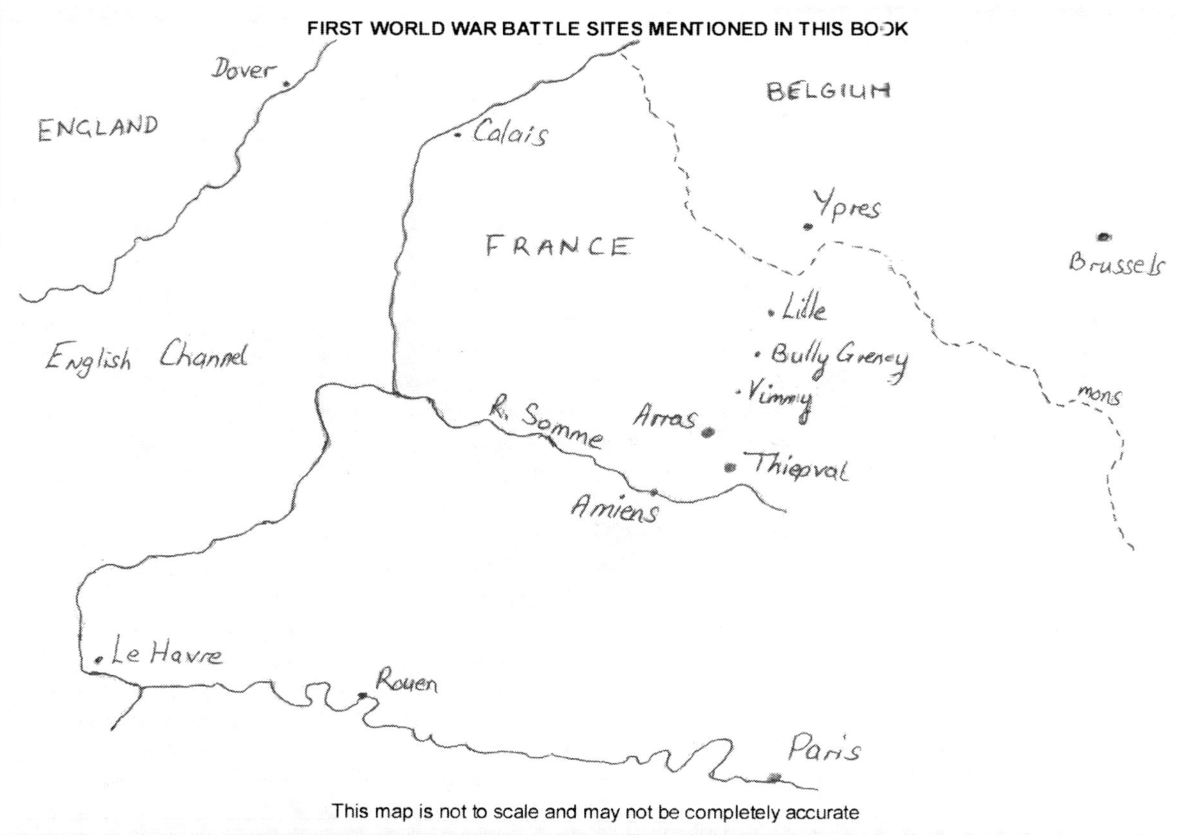

This map is not to scale and may not be completely accurate

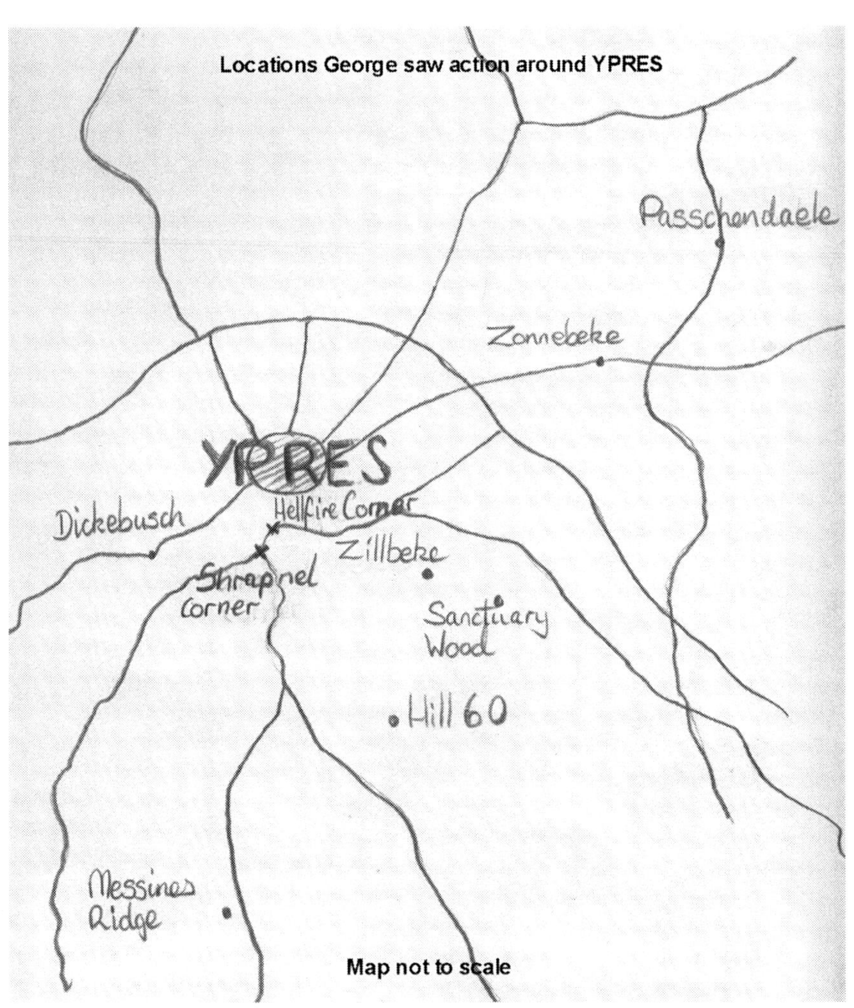
Locations George saw action around YPRES
Passchendaele
Zonnebeke
YPRES
Dickebusch
Hellfire Corner
Zillbeke
Shrapnel Corner
Sanctuary Wood
Hill 60
Messines Ridge
Map not to scale

Chapter 1

Joined Army 1915

In the latter months of 1914, I was following my employment at W.H.Smith & Sons, Waterloo Street, Newcastle Upon Tyne. My wages were 28/- per week for some sixty hours. Having my wife and one child, we had to live sparingly to make things get along sort of "shipshape". In one particular week, I had been absent from my work one day and in consequence, expected my weekly wage to be one day short. The Great War being the main topic these days, I said to my wife as I was leaving for work the day previous to my pay day, "If they keep my day's pay I will go straight and join the Army". Well on payday, I said they had kept off my day's pay and that I had joined the Army. Well, my wife burst into tears and said a whole string of phrases about leaving her with a baby so young, "Georgie two and a half months". She picked up the basket off the chair and hurried out the house, leaving me sitting at the fireside in the dumps as she thought. She went along to my mother's crying and told them I had joined the Army. They all started crying. That same day, I went to my mother's, but I didn't cry, I went laughing and when I told them I hadn't joined the Army, well didn't I cop it.

So it smoothed over eventually and the Great War went on just the same. The newspapers were at this time giving some awful accounts of German brutality towards Belgian and French women and children. At night, when I used to read the paper, I would work myself into a rage thinking of the horrors those poor people were subjected to. Our own soldiers in France were being heavily bombarded with tremendous shells the like of which had never been known before. The King and Lord Kitchener were calling for Volunteers to help their countrymen at the war; thousands were joining day after day for training.

On Monday 3rd of August 1914 Germany declared war on France and as German Armies crossed the Belgian border the following day Germany declared war on Belgium. The British Army mobilised at 4pm that same day and at 11pm invoking the treaty of guarantee which protected Belgium, Great Britain declared war on Germany. The spark that lit this fuse of European self destruction was the assassination of the Archduke Franz Ferdinand, the heir to the Austro-Hungarian throne on 28th June 1914. The build up to the war in Britain and the euphoria and patriotism which greeted this grim news is hard to explain but Britain was a nation proud of its Empire and with its instinctive support for the underdog, thousands rallied to join up within days of the declaration of war. This was fostered by Kitchener's call with the now famous poster "Your Country Needs You". It was a compelling message and led to the establishment of the New Armies that were destined to be the backbone of the British Army at the Battle of the Somme. It was about this time that George first felt the call to arms but thought better of it. But it was only a deferral.

The Britain of those days was very different. Apart from the existence of a strong Empire it was an age of deference to King, the state and the church and all that went with that. All men including George who enlisted in these early days were born in the reign of Queen Victoria. Values of loyalty, discipline and obedience prevailed. Women did not have the vote, boys of 15 were working in the coal pits of Wales and Yorkshire; it was a hard life for those outside the Upper and Middle classes. They were in short, men and women of a different age. The early campaigns in France and Belgium were not the success that the Nation expected. The retreat to Mons had been followed by the Battle of the Marne which threw an over extended German Army off balance and so the race to the sea followed finishing in the last days of October at the Belgian town of Ypres. The first Battle of Ypres was a costly battle with 58,000 casualties and led to the static warfare of the trenches with which the First World War is so much associated.

On 10th March the Battle of Neuve Chapelle commenced. It was an attack by two Army Corps to capture a salient held by the Germans just south of Ypres. Although the attack went well initially it faltered as the British were unable to exploit their success. It was a disappointment and may well have been covered in the newspapers and might have led to George thinking he should do his bit for King and Country. He was to join 315 Brigade RFA, sometimes referred to as 2nd/1st Northumbrian Brigade RFA (TF) which was a Territorial Force artillery brigade formed in 1914 as a second line unit. It was part of 63rd (2nd Northumbrian) Division which was formed in September 1914 for "home service only". 50th (Northumbrian) Division, its first line parent formation, went to France in April 1915 alongside many other Territorial Force Divisions. Lord Haldane established the Territorial Force in 1908 in response to the lessons learnt from the South African War. It was an overdue rationalisation of the old Militias, Yeomanry and Volunteer Corps. Artillery was an important element of the new TF and 315 Brigade was a new unit raised for the duration of the war. The Territorial Force was ostensibly for defence of the homeland but virtually every man volunteered a second time, as it were, to go to France.

On March 27th1915 at 2.00 p.m., I proceeded to the Drill Hall, Barrack Road. I was duly attested, sworn in, made a Soldier of the King and was given three day's leave from the Drill Hall to go home and fix my affairs.[1] After joining the Army, my employers allowed my

1 He was given on enlistment a Regimental Number 1711. This was later changed in 1917 to an Army Number 750610, although his medals (War Medal and the Victory Medal frequently referred to as Mutt and Jeff after

wife 15/- per week for as long as my service lasted, this being a special inducement offered by W.H.Smith to encourage their employees to enlist to serve their country. At the end of my three day's leave, I returned to the Drill Hall, Barrack Road. During my stay there, I was inoculated in the right of my chest and was confined to Barracks for three days whilst the effects wore off. This was done to every man joining the Army, for the prevention of disease. My duty at the Drill Hall was to learn the rough methods of marching, saluting and gun drill, a sort of breaking into Army life in general. After some six weeks of this hum drum life, we were moved to Gosforth Park[2] as the Drill Hall was far too small to accommodate the men who were continually being added to the new recruits.

Gosforth Park was a lovely place to learn soldiering, fine fresh air, pleasant surroundings and quite convenient to the town. Up at the "park" as it was termed by the troops, we were broken in to the more business side and serious part of the Army.

We were at first formed into Batteries, namely First, Second, Third and Fourth and the Ammunition Column.[3] I was picked out to undergo training as a Telephonist and Signaller, but it was a considerable time before I started. Our main work at first was general cleaning up, and then as our horses began to arrive our work was

---

wartime comedians), which are in the family's possession, show his regimental number.

2 Gosforth Park was the local racecourse and was used in both World Wars to train troops. It's the racecourse where the famous Bladon Races was run.

3 George had decided to join the Royal Artillery, which in 1915 had three parts, the Royal Horse Artillery (RHA) who supported the cavalry and therefore travelled faster and had a smaller gun, The Royal Field Artillery (RFA) and the Royal Garrison Artillery (RGA), which dealt with much bigger guns. George was joining the Royal Field Artillery equipped with the 18 pounder quick firing gun. The Royal Field Artillery was organised into Brigades, commanded by a Lieutenant Colonel, with each brigade having four batteries of six guns, commanded by a Major, and an ammunition column. The Fourth Battery in this case D Battery was equipped with six 4.5 inch howitzers. The six guns were arranged in three sections, commanded by a Captain of two guns and each crew of a gun commanded by a Sergeant (No 1) was referred to as a sub-section or just sub for short.

taken up with them. With regards to the guns, all that we had were some twelve old French 90mm, these were mainly for doing drill for officers and all others to get a rough idea of gunnery. The training on these old French guns went on day after day interlocked with horse riding drill. I was engaged in learning the methods of flag signalling, morse code and semaphore with alternating periods of telephone work, laying cables, field wires and going through the outline work of laying telephone and organising systems of flag stations for a battery of field artillery. This was very interesting indeed, not only was it varied and constantly providing changes, but was of great educational value, learning many things one wouldn't have dreamt of in ordinary life. We had many pleasant days doing this sort of work, sometimes being out all day around the surrounding country practising laying cables along the country roads. When I was not engaged in this work, I was busy amongst the rest of my battery, grooming horses, harness cleaning and learning gun drill.

Every morning before breakfast, the rule was to take all horses[4] for exercise. One particular morning, all horses had been saddled up and formed up outside the stables, with the exception of one beautiful grey mare. The sergeant gave this horse to me, saying at the same time, "Here Bombardier[5], this horse wants to be taken out; she's a bit fresh mind". I had a little difficulty in getting her to take the bit, but eventually I got her saddled up with the rest of the ride and was last to leave the stables. On nearing the large field where we exercised them, my horse was lagging behind, despite my efforts to keep her up. She had been a bit frisky during the ride up, but it was nothing out of the ordinary for a fresh horse. All of a sudden, she whipped round and

4 The British Expeditionary Force deployed to France in August 1914 with 120,000 horses and although a large proportion were for the cavalry the majority were used for artillery and the logistic supply of the BEF and as the war went on this dependence on the horse grew. By the end of the war 256,000 horses had perished.

5 It seems that George was given promotion to Lance Bombardier very early on and later he refers to his promotion to Bombardier. He was a promising lad. See Appendix 1 for ranks in the Royal Artillery.

made off back to the stables. I tried all the knacks I knew to bring her to a standstill and after a hard struggle, I succeeded. She was all of a lather and prancing about like a duck on hot bricks, but I calmed her a little and turned her back again towards the exercise field. I got her nicely prancing back again and I was just praising myself on getting her quiet, when she let off a neigh like an elephant, took the bit between her teeth and went off into the field like a racehorse. My horse went pounding like an express train, I tried the same methods to pull her up, recognising that according to Army discipline, I would get punished for galloping a horse unnecessary, but it was to no avail. The horse said "No". I tried sawing at her mouth, which is a crime in the Army, punishable by imprisonment, with the same effect on the horse "nil", I knew then that the best thing to do was to sit tight and let her exhaust herself. We were now about three parts across the field and making towards the rest of the ride. On getting closer, the sergeant major seeing me coming at break neck speed, motioned with his hands for me to pull up, which was impossible. Seeing I didn't do it, he started to canter towards me, now my horse was making a beeline for him. I tried to steer clear by tugging at the reins, but couldn't and just when I thought a collision was inevitable, my horse swerved to the right suddenly and taken unawares, off I came, right among a heap of small ash which had been spread over the grass for a riding school. I had a severe blow on the head, and was very dazed; my face was scratched from the small ash. I was assisted back to billets and next morning was up in front of an officer to give an explanation. My version was accepted and the sergeant was severely reprimanded, for allowing a fresh horse, which had been sick and had had no exercise for weeks, to go out; so ended my first serious baptism into horse management.

After this experience, I was sent to a riding school class, I was really put through it, riding horses bare back, jumping on the horse without stirrups at the standing position, walking and trotting and then cantering, the task was very hard for me and not bad for a novice. I got some very hard knocks with tumbling off, but eventually, practice told its tale. I got practically efficient in horse riding and management, which was to prove a very good friend to me in later years. Matters went pretty well the same for the next few months or so, practical routine work every week with occasional variations of surprise turnouts at different times. This was how the higher authorities found out how the training of officers, men and horses were proceeding. One such instance was as follows, the time 9.00 a.m. one fine morning, we were all busy at our various duties, harness cleaning, grooming and general fatigues, suddenly, officers came to NCO's[6] in charge of different sections with orders. Immediately the NCO's formed their sections into parades and everyone was told to be on parade again in thirty minutes, fully dressed in marching order, with all necessaries to go anywhere for any length of time. At the appointed time, everyone was on parade and formed up in the main road that leads through Gosforth Park. Horses, guns, ammunition, wagons, baggage wagons, officer's carts, cookhouse stores, in fact everything that was necessary and all on wheels ready to move. Commanding Officer Higginbottom[7] inspected the whole brigade on the main road and when he was satisfied that all was correct, he went to the head of the parade and moved off. None of the ranks below Major knew where we were bound for, all were guessing at our ultimate destination, which was later proved wrong. We travelled at a very fast walking pace through Gosforth, down the North Road, Percy Street, Newgate Street, Clayton Street and Scotswood Road, it was when we got near Maiden Street that my horse shied at a passing tram and went onto the footpath just missing Thompson's Newspaper window. When I got him to the road among the rest again, I looked over to Ivy Street and my wife Millie was standing with one of our

6 Non Commissioned Officer

7 Higginbottom was Lieutenant Colonel TA Higginbottom who was a pre war Territorial Force officer in command of a 5th Durham Howitzer Battery based at the Artillery Drill Hall, Ellison Street, Hebburn on Tyne. He was promoted to temporary Lieutenant Colonel on 3 Oct 1915. He was awarded a DSO in 1916 and was made a substantive Lieutenant colonel on 29 Aug 1917. He survived the war.

kiddies in her arms, but she didn't see me. We proceeded at the same fast walking pace along Scotswood Road, past Elswick Station, over the chain bridge and eventually pulled into Axwell Park. We were surprised to see all the artillery that was already congregated. As we were entering the gates we all received the order "Eyes left" and on passing, I noticed a large group of red caps (soldier slang for staff officers), they were viewing us up and down as we passed them. After a stay of two hours or so, to feed and water the horses, we set off, back again, but on a different route. We came over the chain bridge again, turned left and after a quarter of a mile or so, cut off to the right up a big bank and after walking the country roads for some time, we eventually arrived back at the park ready for the stew and barley pudding with figs, which had been prepared for us in our absence. It eventually transpired that the turnout had been a test to find out if the Brigade, in the case of an enemy attack on the coast, could get to an appointed place at an appointed time; the rumour was that we had been forty five minutes late.

We were practically all Northumbrians in the Brigade and on our doorsteps so to speak and according to Army discipline and routine, it was very detrimental to the training of the men, with lateness and absenteeism. Matters were being seriously considered by the CO. Nearing Xmas 1915; we were all packed with luggage, entrained at Killingworth Station and proceeded to York to exchange quarters with a West Riding Brigade RFA, who were under the same disadvantages, namely too near home. Once we were established at York and finally settled down, training in the full sense of the word started in earnest. We were equipped in no time with fresh horses, absolutely spanking new 18 pounder guns from Armstrong's & Whitworth of Elswick including ammunition wagons etc[8]. I was selected to undergo

8 Sir W G Armstrong Whitworth & Co Ltd was a major British manufacturing company of the early years of the 20th century. Headquartered in Elswick, Newcastle upon Tyne, Armstrong Whitworth engaged in the construction of armaments, ships, locomotives, automobiles, and aircraft. For details of the 18 Pound Quick Fire Gun see Appendix 2.

training as a Signaller and Telephonist and was also promoted to Bombardier to take charge of the 1st Battery Signallers.

At the same time as the new guns arrived, I was also handed a full battery telephone and signalling equipment, which included flags for morse code and semaphore, telephones for field work, micrometers and angle of sight instruments, telescopes large and small, field glasses of various sizes and lastly reels of DII and DIII[9] insulated steel wire for field communications. These together formed a rather large amount of valuable property and at the time it amazed me to think that they were all absolutely necessary to carry on with a Battery of RFA in action.

Our billets were situated in a village called Dringhouses about three miles out of York City, quite a lovely little place. My subsection comprising of about thirty six men were all split up into parties of about eight or so, some were billeted in the school, others in private houses in front and back bedrooms which had previously been emptied of their furniture. All other sections of the Battery were similarly placed around villages, so we were quite comfortable at night. We used to get down to York City nearly every night, it being just a penny ride on the tram and many an enjoyable evening we had.

On one particular occasion, a party of six, including me, went out one Saturday night, visited several pubs where there was singing. On nearing the time for making back to billets we were all in the same frame of mind, namely suppertime, "A soldier will always eat". We made our way to a pork shop, where the pea's pudding, pig's trotters, savaloys and black puddings were all in the window, steaming hot; it was a red rag to a bull to us, being half canned. We all bought our stock of eatables, which consisted of an assortment of the above. We boarded a car for Dringhouses and settled down to eat our supper. The tram fairly hummed of pea's pudding etc. In the same car were four Yorkshire Hussars, who are traditionally bitter towards field artillery men. This bitterness set the ball rolling so to speak. One

9 This is two types of signalling wire used for laying line for field telephones.

word led to another, Tyneside slang did not agree with the Yorkshire upstarts, so before one could realise what was wrong, we were fighting. Pea's pudding, black pudding and ducks were all used as missiles, what a mess those Yorkshire Hussars were in. The car pulled up in the main street to stop us, but free fighting carried on in the roadway, then someone shouted "Here comes the MP", everybody scattered and then we dwindled back to billets in two's. The next day York was put out of bounds for a week to our battery, so we paid dearly for our first encounter with the Yorkshire Hussars.

It was the rule in the battery that every morning at 6.30 a.m. all horses had to be exercised. One particular morning, our corporal had charge of our subsection's horses for their exercise. When all horses were mustered in the roadway, they numbered about forty five to fifty, nearly every man had two horses, riding one and leading the other. We had no saddles on, just a bridle and bit, riding bareback. We proceeded to walk to York, going right into the city itself then returned back again on a different route past York Station. Going past the Station, our corporal's horse rather shied at a passing tram and started to make off up the road. I think that he did it purposely with his spurs, as just when his horse bolted, he turned around to us and laughed just as he used to do when he was up to any devilment. His smile and hint was taken up by the rest of the men and everybody made off at a full gallop after the corporal, who by this time was about a hundred yards in front. What a sight it was, nearly fifty horses at full gallop up a main street in a big city like York, passing trams etc, going past carts and people crossing the road, with no semblance of order amongst them. People going to work, mostly girls going to Rowntree's Chocolate Works were all standing looking in amazement; we did cut a sight indeed. Eventually after we had come within a quarter of a mile of our stables, the corporal pulled up his horse and we all stopped. After that, the Police made serious complaints and all exercises had to be done along the country roads.

One good point about this was that we could get to Newcastle pretty easily with a quarter fare Army railway warrant. I may say that these were made use of whenever possible. One difficulty in getting them was that if you were in the sergeant's black books, "Nuff said", you would never get one. Your sergeant had to put your name through to the section officer for a weekend pass, which authorised the holder to be absent from his quarters from 12 mid-day Saturday, until 12 midnight Sunday, in some more lucky cases, it was from Friday 5.00pm. There was never a sufficient number of passes for the men who wished to go to Newcastle. This difficulty made "Tommy" use his wits. What we did was very simple and at the same time very successful. We used to get railway warrants from the battery office in their blank form, from the battery orderly, fill them in with ink and get someone with different handwriting to sign a fictitious officer's name. When going to get the train at the station, we would present it to the booking clerk, thereby obtaining a return ticket to Newcastle, for a quarter of the fare. All that was necessary after that was to dodge the MPs, until the train was about to start, jump in as if in a hurry and all was serene. But all good things have their disadvantage, this one being that you had to be in billets for roll call by 10.00pm. This was sometimes avoided by getting on the right side of your corporal who generally took the roll, to mark you present when you were in Newcastle, likewise for the return on Sunday.

About this time, we had been having some open action drill with all the guns etc, and it was found out during this that the signallers required a lot of training. As there wasn't any competent man in the battery to do this, someone had to be sent away to a school of signalling for expert training and as a result I was chosen. I was sent to Fulford[10], a little village about four miles out of York, where our H.Q. and signalling officer were billeted. I was trained in all branches of signalling and telephony with the H.Q. staff, who were more advanced than us in signalling. One Saturday afternoon after having my dinner, I was getting ready for a trip to York, when I was

10 Fulford, now part of York still has a complex of barracks.

called away to see the signalling officer, Lt. Robinson, who I met in the roadway, beside his private motor car. His first words were "Oh Elder, get your kit packed at once, we are to get the 4.10pm train to Retford, so hurry". It was about 3.20pm and away I went to my billet, wondering why I was going to Retford. I was back beside his car, with my kit ready at 3.35pm, Lt. Robinson's servant brought out his kit a few minutes after and came out looking at his wristwatch, "Jump in Elder", he said, so I got into his motor beside the driving wheel and we set off. As we pulled out onto the main road, he glanced at his watch; it was 3.45pm and a little over four miles to go in twenty five minutes. As he increased speed he said "we'll do it alright". We had been going pretty fast for about ten minutes, when rounding a bend in the road, we saw in front of us a large brewers steam wagon. It was right in the centre of the road, leaving no room at either side to get past. We dashed up to the wagon and slowed down about twenty yards from the rear. The officer was constantly sounding his horn, but the driver of the wagon didn't seem to hear. We couldn't waste any time and were getting anxious about our train. Then suddenly the wagon veered off to the left to allow us past. The officer put on speed and the car jumped forward towards the right side of the road. Just as we were nearly up to the rear of the wagon it edged into the centre of the road again and crash went our cars left mud guard, into the rear of the wagon, buckling it up like paper, then the wagon stopped of course, so did we. There was no time to argue the toss and we eventually got clear and on the way to York again. After the day we had had, the officer just simply let the car rip, going around corners on two wheels. We dashed into York station yard at exactly nine minutes past four; a porter ran up and took our kit with just one minute to purchase tickets and catch the train. The officer got a taxi driver to take his car to the garage and we both ran into the station. He just managed to get into a first class compartment and me a third just as the train left for Retford[11]. We arrived at about 7.00pm, it was a lovely place.

11 In Nottinghamshire just off the A1

On the Monday, both of us were at the signalling school of the RE's[12] and were examined in every branch of signalling and telephony, which lasted until Tuesday night. After tea on Tuesday, the officer came and told me to be ready at 8.30 a.m. on the Wednesday to take the train to Otley. This set me wondering again, why were we going there? When we were both standing on the platform waiting for the train to Otley, I asked Lt. Robinson why we were going, he said that we had to be examined by Royal Engineer Signal Corps to see if we were proficient enough in signalling and telephony before we were allowed to go to Otley, where the main school was. He said we had both passed our exams and were on our way to Leeds, where we would get a local connection for the small town of Otley[13]. We left Retford about 10.00am and arrived at Leeds about 2.00pm, I was fully expecting to get into another train for Otley right away, but no, I got a big shock. I came out of the station with me carrying my kit and two blankets and the officer's valise, so I was wishing we didn't have far to go. We came in to the main street and then along Boar Lane and stopped at the Griffin Hotel, went up the left to the first floor and to the Box Office. The officer went to Register in, put his name down, told me to do the same then he said "Now Elder, we don't go to Otley until tomorrow morning at 9.00a.m., so you can go where you like until then, here's your bedroom ticket, come here and get your tea and supper and meet me at the Station at 8.30 a.m., there's no roll call here". Off he went and left me standing, I was at a loss what to do or say. The waiter, probably seeing my discomfort came and asked me to put my kit in my room, so I jumped at his suggestion for the sake of getting out of sight. I went upstairs, stopped at a room, went in and then the waiter disappeared and I was by myself at last. What a relief. I put my kit down examined the bed, it was nice and soft and springy, I sat on it and then waited. I must have sat there for

12 RE ie Royal Engineers who among other things were responsible for signalling across the Army. The Royal Corps of Signals were not instituted until 1918.

13 Just North of Leeds

about two hours or so, before I plucked up courage to make a move to go out. I came down stairs passing Ladies and Gentlemen in evening clothes with me in khaki and big ruddy boots, I really felt out of place. I went to the box office and was just going down the stairs into the street, when my officer, who had just come out of the dining room, saw me. He made me come back and shouted at a waiter who was going past, then said to me, "tell the waiter what you want for your tea", what a predicament to be in as I didn't know what to ask for. If it had been Lockhart's instead of a big hotel, I could have said it right away, but in the hotel, well, I was just dumb. The officer and waiter couldn't help themselves with laughing, "tell him what you have waiter" my officer said, the waiter turned to me and rattled off such a conglomeration of dishes, that it would have taken a shorthand writer, and linguist to take them down and understand. There was another laugh after that, very much to my discomfort, I felt just like running out into the street. "Would you like some steak and chips Elder", my officer said, "Yes sir", I replied, so it was settled at last. The officer went and the waiter said to me, "Just go into the dining room sir" and off he went; I was once more alone. I went into the dining room, but wanted to come straight out, as the sight that met my eyes, was enough to make anyone in my position feel small. It was a very big room, with small dressed tables, officers of high and low rank sat at various tables, dressed in Army dining jackets. When I entered in my uniform, bandoleer, spurs and cap in hand, they all looked up from their meals and stared at me, I nearly went through the floor and was glad to sit down. Eventually the waiter came in with a large tray, motioned me over to him and then put me at a table in a corner with a screen around, I then felt more at ease. I had steak and chips, coffee, toast, etc, with jellies and fruit for afters and enjoyed it very much. After that I went out into Leeds and had a look around and eventually went to bed about 11.30pm. I had my supper outside in the Y.M.C.A., as I couldn't pluck up courage to go into the Hotel dining room again. I felt more at ease buying my own supper.

Next morning I was awakened by someone knocking at the bedroom door and calling "7.30 Sir". I was up pretty quick and opened the door to find no one there, just a large jug of hot water; I took it, had a good wash and eventually got ready. I went downstairs, not seeing anyone on the way down. I should have gone to the dining room for breakfast, but being self-conscious it stopped me, so I picked up my blankets and kit and went into the street without telling anyone. At about 8.30am I went to a coffee stall on the platform at Leeds station and had a pint of tea and two large buns. Looking over the station square, I saw my officer coming. "Where the hell have you been Elder?" was his first greeting, "I've been looking all over the Hotel for you, had your breakfast yet?" When I told him what I had eaten, he jumped down my neck. "Here's 2/6p, go and get some tuck and be sharp about it". Off I went in the direction of the coffee stall; I stopped there ten minutes, put the 2/6p in my pocket and came back. "Had your tuck?" he asked me," yes I replied, so much for being self-conscious. We eventually got the tram and arrived at Otley at 9.30 am. then took a private car to the signalling school, which was a good half hour's run, it was a lovely drive, all up hill and the scenery was grand. Otley lies in a hollow and the school was right up the slope of the hills.

Altogether I was at the school for six weeks, passing through all the parts of signalling, connected with an army in battle. The most trying test I had was electric lamp reading. The instructors had left the camp some two hours before the test was to begin, in order to get to the signal point, which was six miles across the valley, on the opposite range of hills. When darkness set in, there was a pretty stiff wind blowing across the valley. At the arranged time everyone's attention was drawn to the task at hand. We were told to look for the flash of the electric lamp, on the opposite side of the valley and saw it rattling off the message, in morse code. We were in the darkness, straining to read the message, shouting out the letters to the man behind us, who was writing them down in order to later check the accuracy. We were afraid to wink, on account of mistakes being made when reading the flashes. The lamp was possibly sending the letter T, which in Morse Code, is one long flash of the lamp. By winking your eyes during the flashing of the letter T, one would see two short flashes, with your wink cutting the long steady flash, into two short ones, meant you would read the letter I, instead of T. The strong wind was blowing and with our eyes continually open, water was streaming down our faces. The lamp was the last and practically the hardest test of the whole examination. Eventually the school broke up and we were told which honours we had won. I was awarded a First Class Certificate, having failed to get the highest award of instructor's certificate by three points.

During my six weeks stay at the school, I had two or three weekends at home, by the aid of cheap Army warrants, with fictitious officers' signatures from Friday 5.00pm to Monday 6.00am. Many a good weekend I used to spend at Leeds seeing as much as I could. I arrived back at my battery in York about three weeks before Christmas 1915. With my qualifications in signalling learned at the school, I was able to instruct our signallers in the use of various things such as telephones, switchboards, wire fastening and mending. As Christmas approached, the residents of Dringhouses, led by the vicar, subscribed to a fund to give our battery a real Christmas "tuck in". On Christmas Day we were all taken to the village school and given a right royal feed, turkey, geese, rabbit, pork, Christmas pudding, fruit and even barrels of beer were in abundance, in fact we all feasted ourselves so much that we could hardly move for hours. It was one of the finest Christmas dinners I have ever had. Christmas came and went, and then we all travelled to Strensall Common[14] on the other side of York, what a change it was for all of us. The horses were tied to ropes and stood in the open field all night instead of the comfortable racehorse stables they had left. The men were in tents instead of front and back

14 Strensall has long been associated with the military and is today an Army camp

rooms and everybody had laid down for the night, at about 11.30pm. The alarm bugles were sounded and everybody was turned out of their beds, we were all formed up, just as if it was a daily parade and marched across the common at a very quick pace; it was a good job it was in darkness. It would have been a sight for sore eyes, some with just their shirt on, others with shirt and socks. When we got about a quarter of a mile across the common away from the tents, we were halted and told why it had happened. A German zeppelin had been sighted making for York, hence the necessary precautions to save us from danger. The white tents showed up very clearly at night as well as day and no doubt would make a good target for airship bombs. When we got to know what the trouble was, all eyes were turned up to the sky and sure enough there it was, a large silvery mass moving quickly in the direction of York City. It passed over our tents without any incidents, but it wasn't long before we heard those terrible explosions of large bombs and great glares from the resultant fires. They had dropped them on York City and did extensive damage causing a heavy loss of civilian life. We eventually got back to our tents with our feet all prickles from walking barefoot among the scrub of the common.[15]

Severe training was the order of the day. Us signallers, we were put through it very severely, mainly riding school drill with awkward

---

15 The War Diary of 315 Brigade noted this incident as occurring on 2nd May 1916. L21 was commanded by Kapitanleutnant der Reserve Max Dietrich, the raid only lasting 10 minutes. The approach was made at about 22.30 from Bishopthorpe, dropping eighteen bombs on Dringhouses which injured two soldiers. He then flew over York south west to north east, with bombs falling on Nunthorpe Hall a Red Cross Hospital, as well as Nunthorpe Avenue which killed a girl, injured the spine of her sister and ripped the arm off their mother. A house in Upper Price Street collapsed killing an elderly couple living there. Bombs fell in Caroline Street, and damaged houses in Newton Terrace and Kyme Street, as well as Peaseholme Green which killed five civilians and a soldier and injuring one other, then the other bombs fell in fields outside York, the Zeppelin commander believed he had raided Middlesborough. At the time, York had no searchlights or AA weapons. There was another raid on 25th September by L14 and also on 27/28 November, both in 1916, by L13.

horses. One day a party of twelve signallers, me included, were going through it in the riding school, which was just the ordinary field with a circular track worn by the continual running sound of horses. We had a tree trunk jump rigged up which stood about five feet from the ground and we went over by every possible method known to riding school masters. The sergeant in charge formed us up in front of him to say we were going to be given hell. Every man could testify to this with sore legs and arms. He told us he was very pleased with the way we had gone through the exercises and said "Now lads, just once more for the last!" We all formed up again about fifty yards from the jump, each man had to fold his arms across his chest, take his feet out of the stirrups and let them hang loose by the horse's ribs, get his horse into a full gallop, guide it to the tree trunk, jump over and then gallop back. My turn came, off I went, took the jump, but when my horse was regaining his forelegs on the other side of the jump, I misjudged my time, resulting in me dropping into my saddle. I caught the iron rim at the rear of the saddle with the end of my backbone and was thrown very heavily to the ground, which at this time of year (January) was frozen solid. I was knocked senseless for about a quarter of an hour and eventually carried away to my tent, where I lay for a fortnight before I could sit up.

Strict training in every sphere of artillery work was the order of the day and we had very little time to ourselves. For instance, Reveille was 5.30am, stables at 5.45am to 7.30am then breakfast until 8.15am, parade again at 8.45am until 12.30pm for dinner parade and again at 1.45pm until 5.00pm. We were free to go about camp until 9.30pm, roll call and lights out at 10.00pm; this was our daily routine, not much pleasure. Eh?

Chapter 2

Off to France

In the meantime whilst George was being trained the 2nd Battle of Ypres had been fought. It was an unsuccessful attempt by the Germans to seize Ypres that remained a thorn in their side. Despite the use of gas for the first time their initial successes were not followed up and the uneasy stalemate continued. By now the British had 3 Armies in France and Belgium. However not all was going well and in September 1915 the Battle of Loos commenced as a collaborative plan with the French. It finished with a British loss of 45,000 casualties and little progress was made. In late 1915 allied plans were being made to hold a joint offensive in the area of the River Somme. In February 1916 these plans began to materialise with a meeting between Field Marshal Haig and General Joffre. It was agreed that the offensive would commence on 1 July 1916. A few weeks later after the fateful Battle for Verdun had begun the British Commander-in-Chief agreed to relieve the French 10th Army in the Somme sector. Plans were therefore made to move the 4th Army and for the New Armies, which Kitchener had recruited to assemble for the forthcoming battle. It was this shift of emphasis which undoubtedly led to George and his battery being on the move.

Suddenly without any previous warning, we got our marching

orders, where we were going, no one knew. We were all astir one morning at 4.00am; horses harnessed to the spanking new guns and ammunition wagons. Everybody had to pack all their kit and eventually at about 9.00am after we had had breakfast, we were on the road, bag and baggage. What struck me most from my own observation was the marked contrast there was to a similar bag and baggage parade I have previously mentioned. This early parade saw the men with pale wishy-washy looks on their faces, but this time everyone had that smart soldier like bearing, dark brown faces, bright glossy eyes and above all, that cheesy healthy smile, all of which is only earned by hard work in the open air. We marched along the country road away from Strensall and towards the city of York. When we neared the City, we had the strict order of "Eyes Front". Everyone had to be on their best behaviour, no smoking, and no talking with everyone marching to attention. [16]

On reaching York, we were met by an Infantry full brass band, which formed themselves at the head of the parade, which consisted of the Headquarters' staff, First, Second and Third Batteries and lastly, our Fourth and Fifth Battery and Ammunition Column. The band then struck up playing lively tunes such as Tipperary, Pack up Your Troubles etc. We all felt very important and it was quite evident that crowds of people along the route thought we were going straight to France. With the band still playing, we reached the Station at York. Horses were unfastened from the guns and wagons, scores of men manhandled the guns and equipment into the main entrance of the station onto the platform and then onto the trucks, which were already waiting. Everything was done without a hitch, even the horses were put into the closed truck without serious trouble. The second, third and fourth ammunition columns were entraining at other platforms, which made a total of four trains. After all horses and guns were loaded, the men were paraded and marched to the top of the train, where carriages were waiting, eight men to a

16 The War Diary noted this move as occurring on 17th May 1916.

compartment, which was very uncomfortable. My battery was first to leave, the guard blew his whistle, waived his flag and the express train struggled with the heavy load behind it and we started to move. Into our ears flouted the strain of "Homeland Homeland, When shall I see you again, Land of my birth etc." from the brass band which was perched at the end of the platform giving us a musical send-off. The train gathered speed, the music died away and we were left to our thoughts in a swaying railway carriage, some as happy as could be for the good times we had at York, but alas that feeling of where and what we were intended for came uppermost and eventually the compartment where I was lapsed into silence and I noticed a few moist eyes among the company. As the train gathered speed and started to eat up the miles of track, all of us became jollier and light hearted; our sole interest was in the passing sights of the countryside. We travelled on right through the Midlands and eventually pulled up at Pontefract, where we were all ordered to feed and water the horses. This watering was done with canvas pails pushed from hand to hand and eventually to the horses in the trucks. It was a rather tedious task and in fact, proved to be a waste of time and labour, as the majority of the horses wouldn't drink. We found out in all our later experiences, horses will never drink during a railway journey they had some corn and hay, but only picked at it. When it was all finished and we were ordered back to our carriages, we had a pleasant surprise. All along the platform were women, boy scouts, girl guides and Y.M.C.A men, all with sandwiches of bread and chicken, or chicken paste and great urns of tea, These were given free to any of us who cared to accept them and I don't think anyone refused, they were really welcome, because our rations were only bully beef and dog biscuits. As the main tasks were accomplished, namely attention to the horses and little consideration for the men, off we went again. We went on and on without any further incident, until we pulled up at a wayside station called Codford, on the outskirts of Salisbury Plain, and then we had to work and work hard. All horses were taken out of the trucks, guns were loosened off and after about three hours graft, we were on the road again. After about eighteen hours on the train, we eventually arrived at a camp[17] on Salisbury Plain and were put into our respective billets.

The next morning was devoted to getting everything ship shape. After we had settled down and got used to our surroundings, we were put through the most rigorous training I have ever endured. Every day we were out with the guns, on the large open plains, miles from anywhere. Galloping here, there and everywhere and halting every now and again. We put the guns into action, firing blanks, hitching the guns up again and after the supposed enemy. We continued all day with only bully and biscuits and water for our meals, although, after we arrived back at camp, we always had some lovely stew and rice. After the food we were ready for our bed, which consisted of two small trestles about three feet long and six inches high, with three long planks of wood to lie across the two trestles. There was a large canvas oblong bag, filled with straw for the mattress. We had two blankets, our own overcoats and when all were put together, we were quite comfortable in the large hut. On other days, we signallers were out in a body, under R.E. Signal Officers, doing very strict training and had some very good and bad days. Sometimes we would be out all day in pouring rain, wet to the skin, but still carrying out the training. During training, I had a horse called Peter who was a lovely chestnut whom I was very attached to. I could get the horse to do practically anything I required. There were occasions when it was necessary for me to leave him standing in a small wood, or near a hedge, while I was some distance away, signalling to my comrades in the distance, had a horse been with me, I would have been spotted by the supposed enemy. A horse that wasn't trained, who wouldn't stand by himself, would be back to his stable in quick time, but Peter would be there, when I came back to him. If the occasion demanded it, I would whistle, or shout and he would come trotting whilst munching

17 The camp they arrived at was Heytesbury just outside Warminster. It is probably on the site of the current camp now called Knook Camp.

a mouthful of grass. A horse of his kind was a necessity to a signaller, as they often had to be left.

After about a couple of months of training in everything relative to open action warfare, we were all prepared for a gunner inspection and examination by the higher command from the War Office, this meant that if we all passed, we were meant for France, as soon as possible. The day of examination arrived and the entire brigade, consisting of some twenty four guns, was mustered at the artillery shooting range, in the middle of Salisbury Plain. A squad of redcaps, generals and staff officers etc came up. Each battery was tested separately at the range and because we had never seen a gun actually fired, or a real shell burst, we were all excited. It was a very interesting day for us all. All the rank and file and a large percentage of officers passed through the strict test.[18]

After we had been in camp for about a fortnight, we were all told that every man would get ten days leave to go home before we went overseas. We were sent off home in batches, when one batch came back, another went and so on, right through the brigade, until every man had his leave. I had my leave at about the third batch and was really pleased to see my wife and kiddies again. I had a right royal time at home, for I was going to "France at last", what an honour to be proud of. Time goes on, so on the Sunday we left from The Central Station at 12 noon. What a leave it was, wives, sweethearts, mothers and fathers, all on the platform, soldiers, laughing and joking to keep our spirits up, vaguely realising that this parting might be the last for some of us. The whistle blew and the train started to move along, there was much weeping among the women-folk and even among the soldiers. Amid the hum of the revolving wheels and the creak of the train, there rose that now famous song "Homeland", from the soldiers. We left Newcastle, not to see it for two long years, time that proved to be the ageing of mind body and soul.

18 The War Diary states that the Brigade was inspected by the GOC RA on 22 May.

After we were back to camp, we were privileged with late passes to Warminster, about four miles away; this privilege was very often used. My pal Michael Kinney, another chum called Bentley[19] and I had some jolly nights at Warminster in the pubs. We were enjoying ourselves as much as we could, knowing that we wouldn't have much more time in old England.

At last, on 25th June 1916[20], we entrained at Codford and proceeded to Southampton, arriving there at 4.30pm with the train running alongside the ship. We immediately started to put the horses on board. The guns and wagons were being put aboard and eventually after about two hours every one was on the ship below decks. We left the Southampton Dock, without so much as a cheer, slowly and silently, just as if we were afraid of being seen; what a contrast to our previous send-offs. We steamed out of harbour and anchored in Southampton, waiting for darkness before proceeding to the English Channel. When darkness came, the ship started off at full speed. When we were in dock we could see through the darkness, four shadowy shapes of torpedo boats circling around us time and time again. This was our escort to protect us from German submarines.

19 Gunner WA Bentley did not survive the war, he died on 28 November 1918 after the Armistice, possibly of influenza. He is buried in the Awoingt British Cemetery just outside Cambrai. He was married. George makes no mention of his mate dying probably because he was in hospital himself at the time. He crops up elsewhere in the story.

20 The War Diary notes that this move occurred on 2 July. At that time the Brigade comprised of 26 Officers, 581 Other Ranks and 513 horses. George as part of A Battery sailed on the SS Anglo Canadian.

Chapter 3

Somme 1916

George was probably unknowingly involved at this time in an interesting military reorganisation. In 1914 surplus manpower in the Royal Navy were formed into a division to fight as an Army formation although remaining under the control of the Royal Navy. Winston Churchill, as First Lord of the Admiralty, was the architect of this unusual arrangement and took special interest in its activities. Removed from their natural element to fight as infantry, they nevertheless retained their original ranks and named their battalions after distinguished naval heroes such as Anson, Drake, Hawke, Hood, Howe and Nelson. Only the British could possibly entertain such an arrangement! At first it was deployed largely untrained and ill equipped to Antwerp in 1914 and in 1915 it fought at Gallipoli, that ill fated campaign that was also the brainchild of Winston Churchill. In May 1916 the Royal Naval Division arrived in France from the Mediterranean and was reinforced to the strength of an Army Division. However there was a price to pay the Division had to pass from the control of the Navy and the Admiralty to the Army and the War Office. The Royal Naval Division had no integral artillery so all the artillery of the 63rd (2nd Northumbrian) Division was transferred. The other Brigades and units of the Northumbrian Division were dispersed amongst other Army divisions and the Royal Naval Division was renamed the 63rd (Royal Naval) Division.[21]

As dawn approached, all hands were ordered to put on life jackets and thanks to the British Navy, we sailed into the harbour of Le Havre at exactly 8am. All eyes were eagerly scanning the shore, trying to see as much of France as they could for the first time. We passed into the inner harbour slowly, because of the French minefields in that locality and I noticed that stretching the full breadth of the harbour was a boom. This consists of large tree trunks bound securely together, floating on the surface of the sea. They were laying about eight or ten alongside each other and in the centre of this boom was a narrow passage, which was the only safe entrance to the inner harbour. This boom was a sure protection against the German submarines getting into the inner harbour, amongst the shipping. Tragic evidence of this was glaringly exhibited before our eyes, large numbers of big and small ship masts and funnels, just protruding above the surface of the sea, outside the boom, this clearly showed what damage the submarines had done. German submarines had sunk these ships, while trying to enter the harbour of Le Havre. We eventually moved into one of the large inner docks, of which the harbour abounds and started to disembark. This was a rather gruelling task compared to the embarking at Southampton, whereas at the other port, there was plenty of room, it was very congested at Le Havre. After much army cursing and hard work, we got everything off the ship and were all formed up in parade order. Crowds of French people were viewing us from head to toe, laughing and shouting, which was a jumble of words to us, all we could do was laugh. If some of the soldier's expres-

21 63rd Divisional Artillery consisted of 315, 317 and 223 Brigades RFA. Brigadier-General AH de Rougemont was appointed Commander Royal Artillery and remained so throughout the war. He had two sons one of which, Michael, whilst serving in the Grenadier Guards was killed in North Africa in World War 2. Lieutenant Colonel Higginbottom was the Commanding Officer of 315 Brigade and was therefore George's CO.

sions had been understood by the French crowd, well enough said. We moved off at about 3.00pm, passing through the large wide main streets, seeing many things that were new to us. It was nearly dusk, when we pulled into a camp, which had obviously been used only recently because various army belongings, were scattered around stables and huts. This gave us the impression that whoever had been there previously, had left rather hurriedly, probably to make room for us. After the horses had been fed and watered, they were loosened out of the Guns and Wagons, but were in the stables with their harnesses still on, we were told to rest the best we could. There was no going to the City of Le Havre, "oh no", we just had to wait.

It was about 1.00am, we were all busy again getting ready for the road. This didn't take long, as everybody was very tired and on edge as we had hardly had any rest or sleep for thirty six hours, since leaving Southampton. Coupled with this, the dismal surroundings of the place we were in, made men want to get away from it, anywhere, it didn't matter where service was.

Off we went once again, everyone from Tom, Dick and Harry saying, "Where the hell are we going to now", "I'm not half tired", "damn the war" etc. These are a few sample expressions from the men as we were marching along behind the guns and wagons. There were no lights in the City with no one about, apart from French soldiers and police who made it more miserable and nerve racking. After half an hour's travel, we entered a large goods station next to the civilian railway station. We pulled up alongside a large train of cattle and ordinary trucks and there was more hard work in getting everybody on board. There was no platform, only the ground on a level with the railway lines, so one can imagine what work was entailed in getting heavy 18 pounder guns and wagons into trucks that stood about six feet from the level of the ground. It was in the early hours of the morning and it was dark, so we had a good opportunity for dodging the column, soldiers' slang for dodging the work. We could easily get into a truck and sit and smoke, while others were grafting. Eventually we were all ready on board, horses were in cattle trucks, men were in ordinary closed-in goods trucks and officers were in passenger coaches. Officers came along and ordered us to see if everything was O.K, with sergeants calling their subsection rolls to see if everyone was present. After that operation was completed, we moved off slowly at about 3.00am, little did we think how long and tedious this journey was going to be.

As dawn broke, we could see the countryside stretching for miles on either side, with not the slightest sign of war. Our train jogged along at about fifteen miles per hour, it was going so slow that some of the men were getting off to pick flowers, or pinch some turnips or apples from the fields and orchards. On some occasions when we passed through a town, it was quite a feature to have youngsters running alongside the trucks, shouting in broken English words they had picked up from English soldiers, who it seemed had passed this way before." bully beef, bully beef," they would shout, until some soldier would shout to them and without any hesitation they would shout back.

We had many stops during the journey, mainly to feed and water the horses. As far as the men were concerned, our old favourite was good enough, bully and hard tack. We had been issued with dry tea and sugar, with one tin of ideal milk between twenty-five of you at the outset of the journey. It was all right in its place, but on a train journey, none of us could appreciate it, owing to the absence of boiling water. Then Tommy's wits came once more to the rescue. When the train was going slow, we would put some dry tea and sugar in our mess tins, jump off, run up to the engine and shout to the driver. Having attracted his attention, we would point to our tin, and then to a pipe at the side of the engine which hot water was coming from. The driver, knowing what we meant, would turn on the hot water and we were able to have our tea. Of course as others saw us, there was a raid on the engine, if the driver had supplied everyone, he would have run out. We were all weary of the constant journey we took every day, since leaving Salisbury Plain. Some of us tried to snatch some rest on the floor of the truck, but it was next to impossible with forty men all shouting. As darkness set in and nothing could be seen or gained by looking out, the doors were closed, candles were lit by those who had them and the majority of us lay down, to get some sleep.

We were all rudely awakened by the stopping of the trucks and the shouting of the N.C.O. It was still quite dark, raining and with a stiff wind. What struck us most was the constant boom, boom, of the guns and the flashes lit up the sky, what a sight to us who had never seen the likes before. Right along the skyline as far as the eye could see, was flash, flash, flash with red and yellow colours and the dull roar of the guns along with it. We all thought we were right into the war with some of us fully expecting to have shells drop among us, there and then. The unloading of the train went on and eventually after about three hours work, everyone was in the mood once more. We marched for about another hour and then pulled into a field to set up camp; this consisted of tents for men and fields for horses. At night we had a look around to get some idea of our whereabouts. We got off the train at Pernes[22] in the Somme district, it was only a small French village and it was there that we had our first interviews with the "Frenchies". What a scream it was, to see and hear men trying to make the French women understand what they wanted. It was though surprising how quick one had an insight into the language to make oneself understood regarding eatables. We remained at Pernes, doing the same training as we did at Salisbury Plain.

After about a fortnight we set off once more arriving at Verquin[23]. While we were there, we could see by the signs that we were not far from the guns, large dumps of shells of all sizes were lying by the roadside and close by there were bales of barbed wire by the trenches. To make us more certain we were near to war, we eventually saw

22 Not actually in the Somme District but West of Bethune and closer to Loos.

23 Just south of Bethune.

large and small batches of Infantry in battle order, going towards the "line" (trenches).

One night about six o'clock, nearly all our gunners and signallers, were told to pack up our kits and parade. When all had mustered we marched away on foot. After about an hour or so of passing ruins on the way, we came to a village called Bully Grenay[24]. This village was pretty intact, that is to say the masonry of the houses was barely harmed by shellfire. Some houses were raised to the ground, where a direct hit had taken place, but the majority were more or less untouched. Large numbers of shops were open, displaying their goods, such as silk shawls and sweets and chocolate etc. We were all surprised, to see such a display in what we understood to be the "war area", or danger zone. We left the main street and proceeded down what I would call in English, "a back lane", the end of which terminated in a large field. There in this field, to our intense amazement, were six-gun pits, each of them containing an 18 pounder gun. This was our first sighting of the British Artillery in the Great War. We were eventually distributed to these six guns, in equal numbers. We signallers were sent to the dugout, where all telephone communications were made. Gunners of the 47th London Division already manned the guns and it was to this particular division that we had been sent to get instructions and an insight into being in action. After a good deal of instruction in telephony and wire laying by the Sergeant Signaller of the battery, I was instructed by my O.C. to take charge of everything. The men, who had been at the guns before we came, left in a body, taking with them only their personal belongings, kit etc., and we were left in possession of everything else. I later learnt that they proceeded to our wagon Line at Verquin and took over our spanking new 18 pounder guns[25] we had brought from England.

---

24 A village very near the battlefield of Loos. The War Diary lists this move as taking place on 15th July.

25 The War Diary notes that the new 18 pounder guns were handed over on 25th July.

My first experience in action[26] was very interesting, as it gave me a good outline on how the war was going. Every morning, it was my duty to inspect my telephone wires, which were laid over the surface of the ground. The infantry wire was pegged into the sides of the trenches with staples. One of my wires was laid over ground for four and a half miles, to what we called the "Oh Pip", meaning observation post. This particular place was always as near to the German trenches as possible, because it was from this spot that an officer would look through field glasses at the German Lines to get information, or spot targets such as parties of Germans in trenches, patching up the damage our guns had done to them the previous night, or spotting some German transport proceeding along the road further to the German rear. In such cases as these, our officer would immediately speak down our telephone wire to our guns and tell them to open fire. The result, more often than not there was nothing left where the Germans once stood, this was a daily occurrence.

One particular incident in connection with this "Oh Pip"[27] very nearly ended with taking three of us to "Kingdom Come", namely an officer named Lt. Brown[28], Bombardier Elder and Gunner Jobey. All three of us were at the "Oh Pip" for a period of four days at a stretch with our rations for this period. The "Oh Pip" was just like a little hut built into the side of a trench, with a small spy hole looking directly on the German trenches, which were about three hundred yards away in the valley. Our officer had a large military telescope, the end of which was protruding slightly through the spy hole to enable him to focus it upon the enemy helmets. His particular work on this occasion was to note their shelling of our trenches. The day was lovely and fine with sun shining bright. Our officer casually remarked that Jerry had dropped two high velocity shells in the valley. I looked out of the spy hole along with the officer and we saw another two shells a little bit nearer to us, it was getting interesting. One officer

26 The Battery went into action for the first time on 18th July.

27 Observation Post

28 Lieutenant NS Brown, later to be Adjutant of 315 Brigade.

remarked to us "I wonder if the "B" is ranging on us", he no sooner got the words out of his mouth, than crash, bang, such a row I had never heard before, dust and lumps of earth were falling upon us. We scattered along the trench as fast as our heels could touch the ground. As we were running, we heard another two swishes over our heads, but well away from us, we stopped panting about fifty yards away. "That was a close one boys", our officer said laughing, we came back after he stopped shelling and what a mess met us. The opposite side of the trench to our "Oh Pip" door had completely caved in and blackened, just as if someone had poured pails full of ink over the disturbed earth. Judging from where the shell had struck the trench side, we came to the conclusion that it had just missed the corner of our spy hole by about a foot. It buried itself into the opposite side of the trench and being of a soft nature, rather subdued the resultant explosion. If the shell had hit the "Oh Pip" or if the trench side had been hard, we couldn't have escaped the contents of it, which would have meant "Nappo". This incident was only a forerunner of what I was later destined to experience, it also gave me a slight insight into what our original expeditionary force had to experience without any protection.

Another feature of this district I will never forget is the drinking water, which was available for our soldiers at the "Oh Pip", only on production of a pass issued by the General Officer Commanding the Sector authorising the bearer to obtain water. It was clear spring water from the bottom of a range of hills called Notre Dame De Lorette[29], on which the "Oh Pip" was situated. The water that trickled out of the earth had been artificially directed into large concrete tanks, over which had been placed great iron covers just leaving sufficient space to get the water out. The utensil used for this purpose was a large biscuit tin with handles. These tanks were surrounded by barbed wire entanglements, in about six rows that stood twelve feet high,

29 Situated just North of Arras Notre Dame de Lorette is a range of low hills which is now the largest French Memorial of World War I. The French fought a series of battles here between October 1914 and March 1915,

there was only one access to this enclosure, which was a doorway through the wire about the breadth of a man. Standing at this door was a soldier with rifle and fixed bayonet permanently on guard, all of which goes to prove how valuable it was. This was the best I have ever tasted, nice and crystal clear, good even to look at with a nutty flavour. The only drawback was it had to be collected at night, because it was under direct observation of the Germans. The enemy could not have known there was a water tank because the foliage of the large trees, which grew on the hillside, hid it and no one had to approach during daylight under any circumstances.

My brother Jack was in an anti-aircraft section of the R.A. and from previous letters I had received from him when I was still in England, I knew he was in this district. From a code we had devised between us, we could each let each other know where we were. He told me in a letter that he was in a place called Verquin. As soon as the opportunity arose, I obtained leave, and set off on a horse to find him, as we had never met in France. Because we hadn't seen each other for eighteen months, I was rather excited to get the opportunity. I arrived at Verquin and after several enquiries, I was very disappointed to find he had left the district the previous day for Vermelles, so it was not to be and I returned very dejected.

After about three months in the position at Bully Grenay, we were told to prepare to move and pulled the guns out of the pits to set off on the road once again. Several days later, I received a letter from Jack telling me he had heard about my seeking him and immediately left Vermelles to see me at Bully Grenay, only to meet with the same disappointment. We arrived at our wagon line on the same day as we pulled the guns out of action; we stayed there overnight and left the next morning. We marched away from the firing line and stopped at Roellecourt[30], a village six miles from the large town of St. Pol. Our title was changed from 315th Brigade R.F.A. to 315th Brigade.

30 The War Diary states that A Battery went to the village of Roellecourt on 23 September.

R.N.D.A.(Royal Naval Divisional Artillery).[31] This Naval division had landed in France from Gallipoli and the Dardanelles. They had no artillery of their own so we were attached to act with them in action. We were billeted a few miles away to undergo very severe training for a big attack on the Germans in the near future.

After three weeks of hardships i.e. not seeing a bed for nights, sleeping in fields behind hedges, and short rations etc., we were taken back to our billets to pull ourselves together. We had a rather easy time with good rations and a good deal of freedom at night and this was utilised up to the very last minute. The pubs were frequented for their wines, obtained pretty cheaply giving rise to many a drunken night. A party of four of us set off at 5.00pm to go to St. Pol about six miles away on "Paddy's Pony". Having arrived there about 7.00pm we made a round of the pubs, finishing up at about 9.30pm at a pork shop. Each of us had a small bottle of champagne and a large polony type of savaloy and a loaf, or I should say cake of French bread, which was like our English brown. As we walked back, we were in a pretty poor state, with still six miles to go to our billets. Further description is hardly necessary, only to say that I can't remember for the purpose of this record, the time it was we arrived.

One day, while I was doing my ordinary duty at our wagon line, I had a rather serious accident. We had all been attending to our horses, cleaning them etc., when at feeding time, I got kicked. We had one horse with odd eyes, one silver eye and the other dark, and the troops nicknamed him Fagi. Everyone knew what sort of horse he was and gave him a wide berth; he would kick his full force at anything and was kept apart from other horses. At feeding time, it is practically essential that all horses are fed at the same time, to stop the kicking and biting. Mr Fagi, standing alone, with his head tied to a long rope, was waiting for his nosebag, which was lying on the ground a few yards away. All the other men were occupied, so I picked up Fagi's bag to put on his head and being fully alive to his bad habits, I walked away

31 This change took place sometime earlier than George states.

from him to the rope, I stood dead in line with his head, about ten yards away, I walked slowly up to him, keeping well away from his rear. I got about three yards away, just close enough to enable me to get hold of the string of the bag, ready to loop over his head, when he let out such a pull, he swung his hind legs around and let out with all his force at me. One of his hind hoofs caught me just below my right kneecap. I went down shouting with pain and was carried away to my billet to be examined by our doctor, who ordered complete rest. He said I was lucky not to have a broken leg. How that horse had swung his hind legs around at such an angle I can't understand. I was laid up for three weeks before I was able to work. I got my own back on Mr. Fagi when I was on night guard. There was not a kick left in him, after me and two other men were finished, he eventually proved to be so dangerous he was taken to be shot and so ended Mr. Fagi.

During these little adventures, all the men, guns and other equipment were examined from time to time by Generals and staff officers and it was quite evident to all that there was something in the wind. In the course of a few days we were once again on our way, marching through St. Pol and several other towns, eventually arriving in the Somme district. We stopped at Englebelmer[32] to rest for a few days, because the march from the St. Pol district had worn us out. The next night, all gunners and signallers with equipment, set off at dark towards the line (trenches). My best mate Michael Kennedy and I were sitting on top of an ammunition wagon with our backs to the horses. As we travelled along the roads, we could see what a state the country was in, shell holes were everywhere, some new, others not. The roads were practically impassable for anyone on foot; even our horses had great difficulty at times in making headway. The roadway was swimming with thick mud, about six inches deep. Darkness came all too soon, making progress even more difficult. With traffic coming towards us and others in front continually halting and moving on

---

32 Englebelmer is a village in the Department of the Somme, 8 kilometres north-west of Albert and 24 kilometres south-south-east of Arras.

again, it made one very rattled. A shout would break the spell, "Gunner, leg over" meaning that some of the horses legs had got entangled with the traces[33], causing it to kick and fling about, so the gunners had to dismount to put matters right. This was done in pitch darkness, the only lights to be seen were the far distant Verey Lights[34] of the trenches or someone on the guns or horses lighting a fag or pipe. After about two hours of this horrible travelling, we suddenly came to a halt; Michael and I were still sitting on top of the ammunition limber; we could only see each other by the glow of the "fags" in our mouths. In our ears was the continual ear splitting reports of our guns firing and the sound of large shells gurgling through the air, over our heads from our big guns right behind us. We had just started to wonder and talk about what the cause of the stoppage was, when "Whiz Bang, Whiz Bang" accompanied by the bright yellow flash and ear splitting explosion which came suddenly to our eyes and ears. It was in front of us down the road, where I judged the foremost of our battery would be. They were German high velocity shells bursting along the roadway and some just about six feet above. We could see by the flash and the bursts that they were getting nearer to us. Realising our danger, I shouted "Put your tin hat on Mick" at the same time jumping from the ammunition limber to the ground with Michael doing the same. We had just got to the ground and hadn't even got our tin hats on, when there came such a report and a flash light over our heads, it was blinding and deafening at the same time. All I could remember immediately after, was staggering across the road through the mud and hearing a confused sound of galloping horses, men shouting, shells bursting and after that, clank, clank and

33 The trace is the steel cable bound in leather which connects the team of horses to gun and limber. To drive the traces should be taught but when slack a horse can get his leg over, leading to the cry "leg over" when all comes to a halt to put this right.

34 The Verey pistol which fired flares for illumination or signalling owes its origin to Edward Wilson Verey (1847–1910), an American naval officer who developed and popularized the device. It was still in service with the British Army in the 1990s.

blackness deeper than night. I came to my senses, seemingly hours after, but in reality only about fifteen minutes. I was lying close to a hedge side, my head was dizzy, thumping and throbbing, I hardly realised where I was or what I was doing. I remember putting my hands to my temples and feeling it sticky. As I was gradually coming to, I started to make my way towards the sounds of horses galloping and the noise of wheels and men with shells still dropping all over the place and I could see by thin vivid flashes and explosions. I reached the roadway and stood a while to find out where my battery was, but they were not there, so I was at a loss what to do. Various men and wagons went past through the darkness, I endeavoured to ask them who they were, but they either didn't see or hear me, then suddenly during a lull in the awful din, I heard a familiar voice calling out in agonising tones, "Kid, Hi Kid, Geordie, Oh Geordie", I immediately recognised my pal's voice, it was Michael Kennedy, who had previously been sitting in the ammunition wagon with me, so I set off across the road in the direction of where I heard him calling from. At the other side of the road, I fell into a large ditch full of mud and slime, which drains of the roadway during wet weather. I pulled myself out and scooped as much of the mud off as possible with my hands. In the darkness, I went over a field and immediately saw a dim shape lying on the ground a few yards away. Here was my pal Michael and another man from our battery. Michael was still shouting "Kid, Kid, Geordie, Geordie" and did all the time until I came towards him. I struck a match and saw he had been hit with something on the muscle of the left upper arm and his topcoat sleeve was wet and sticky. When I spoke to him, he seemed to recognise me, but often went delirious again, shouting for me and then laughing and crying alternately. I recognised that he must be severely wounded and took steps to save his blood and his life. I cut his topcoat sleeve off, taking no notice of the way he was shrieking and crying I had to set my teeth against the sound of screaming shells which were hurtling through the air, dropping into the field where we were. Michael had a lanyard over his shoulders, the regulations were for one on the right arm, but Michael also had one on the left to act as a watch chain. I tied it around his arm between the wound and his shoulder bone, pulling it as tight as I could. He screamed, but I knew it was for the best; he then lapsed into a sort of coma from loss of blood and still kept mumbling, "Kid, kid, Geordie, Geordie". I then got hold of his back as best I could. The other fellow had his feet, but when we moved him, the poor chap let out some of the most awful yells and screams I have ever heard, or ever wish to hear again. As we couldn't move him, I started looking for assistance, but it was very foolish at the time, as I didn't know where we were or where to look for anybody in the dark. Then luck or providence stepped in; I came across a trench board by kicking it with my feet as I was groping across the field. Realising that this would act as a stretcher, I dragged it to Michael. We got him on to it with more shouting from him and walked across the field towards the roadway. The ditch, which I previously fell into, gave us a good deal of trouble, but we managed. Various wagons were still intermittently galloping along the road, but going too fast for us to stop them. We were looking for a First Aid Post, but which way to go, right or left, we couldn't say. We eventually chose right, which turned out to be the correct way. I was feeling faint and exhausted from the excitement and my head was throbbing. After staggering along the muddy road in total darkness, I suddenly saw a bright light from a doorway of a dug-out which was in a little sunken roadway that led off the road; it was about six feet or more below the level of the fields at either side. We got up to the doorway to see little Red Cross Ford cars standing close by the side. I entered the doorway first, with Michael's head behind me. The dugout was an Ambulance Port lit up with acetylene lamps, which made it as light as day. I saw several doctors, one said "put him on here Laddie", pointing to a couple of trestles. I turned around and with the other fellow, put the trestle board which he was on, to the trestles. Suddenly, the doctor, Michael, trestles, and lights started to go around and we were suddenly in total blackness, I had fainted. When I came around, I was half lying on a form[35] with an enamel bowl of Oxo in my hand; my head was thick with bandages. I had a faint recollection of getting a blow on the head when the shelling first started. I called the doctor and asked him what was wrong with my head, "Well Sonny" he said smiling", your right temple has been hit with a piece of shell and whatever it was it hit you flat and you are more burnt than cut, if it had hit you edgeways, well, you wouldn't be here. I was kept in the ambulance post and was sitting on the form having my Oxo, when I saw the stretcher bearers of the R.AM.C.[36] carrying my pal Michael out from the shelf he had been on after they had attended to his wounds. I immediately went over and spoke to him, but Michael was dead to everything, which was going on. The lad had been dosed up to ease his pain and went away without recognising me. He was put into an ambulance car and taken away further to the rear and eventually to England, never to return to France.[37]

On that same day, I left the ambulance post and proceeded to find my battery I eventually found them on the slope of a hill, already established in gun positions. I reported to my C.O. and was immediately given knowledge of my signal communication wires etc. and who was connected with me on the phone. I was given a list of secret code words and abbreviations, this was a regular procedure at every new gun position the Battery took up and I was always strictly ordered to immediately identify all code words and abbreviations in case they ever got into enemy hands.

Practically every man had newspapers and parcels sent to them from home, the parcels of edibles used to come in very handy to supplement our rations. Every night when the rations for the battery came up from the rear, there was a great deal of excitement among the men, but there was disappointment when no mail arrived. The

35 I have no idea what a "form" is, it seems it is a sort of bench.

36 Royal Army Medical Corps

37 As he is not listed on the Commonwealth War Grave list of those who died in WW1 one presumes he survived.

newspapers we received were a week or so old, we read a particular speech of Lloyd George; he remarked that by October 1916 we would have the guns wheel to wheel in France. This speech proved to be true on the Somme where we were. The guns were not actually wheel-to-wheel, but as near to each other so that firing could be carried out with reasonable safety, they were also far enough apart to minimise the risk of being hit by enemy shells.

Every night, all officers and our battery watches were synchronised, the correct time was sent over phones from Brigade Headquarters at the rear. The importance of this was vividly shown to us all. Every morning at about 5.30 a.m. while it was still pitch dark and fairly quiet, apart from machine gunfire in the trenches and occasional shells bursts around the batteries and roadways, the officer whose turn of duty it was went up to the guns and roused all the gun men and gave them one order "Action". Every man would jump to his particular post on the gun. The officer would be standing in the centre of the six guns, watch in hand with his little electric torch shining on its dial. His voice would ring out clear:- "Ready, One, Two, Three, Four, Five, Six!", the time was then 16 minutes to 6 and as the large hand of the officer's watch came exactly to a quarter to six, his voice would ring out loud and clear "Guns Fire". They would then let the shells rip as fast as they could fire; this went on for exactly fifteen minutes and stopped dead on 6 o'clock. Every gun, large and small in the vicinity of the battery, carried this operation out to the second. I later learned it was also carried out on our Somme Front for a length of about fifteen miles. This little bombardment of the German trenches was made every morning from 5.45 am to 6.00am for exactly a fortnight. When our guns finished, Mr Fritz would start retaliating, but only for a few minutes or so. With these regular bombardments, we could easily see if a big attack by our troops was impending, as the object was to put the Germans on edge and keep them in a state of uncertainty. They also realised that something was afoot, but they couldn't guess the day or time, therefore as each of our bombardments took place, they naturally looked for our troops going over the top. They eventually took the necessary precautions such as having more soldiers in their trenches to repel an attack; this gave our guns better opportunities to cause more casualties.

One evening I was sent to the C.O.'s dugout, when I arrived I saw one of our section officers, my C.O. said he had chosen us to go forward with the Infantry, to act as liaison officer and signaller between the infantry and artillery in our respective sections. The liaison officer of the artillery brigade had to be present with all the infantry when they went over the top to ensure that the guns would fire on the necessary targets which the infantry commander desired. We were told that Zero hour was 6 o'clock the following morning; therefore we had to go up the trenches immediately to get the lay of the land and some knowledge from the respective infantry officers whom we were to be working with. At about midnight, the officer and myself went away from the battery to proceed to the trenches, my sole equipment consisted of tin hat, gas mask, a reel of thin telephone wire, telephone earth pin on my leg and a couple of signalling flags. My officer had his maps, tin helmet, gas masks, revolver and cartridges. Zero hour denoted the exact time the attack would take place. We reached the trenches and proceeded by a zigzag route up to the third reserve line, this was the third line of trenches from the Front. We had nothing of importance to note on the way up. I connected my battery to the side of the trench and conversed with Company Headquarters. I was on the lookout for any breakages and finding a few I immediately put them right. We reached the reserve line, then my officer went to a dugout and ordered me to follow him, it was about fifty feet deep with a great number of rooms at the bottom. I was sent to the signallers' room where the Infantry and Royal Engineer Signal Corps were busy on the phones. I reeled off part of my wire and connected the end to the infantry phones. I turned my phone on and told my signaller at the battery that my officer and I had arrived safe and sound. During this time my officer was in the infantry officers' quarters getting his instructions, the time was then about 2.30 am and as the attack didn't take place until 6.00am, I decided to have forty winks in a snug corner and immediately went to sleep. When I awoke, there was a continuous dull drumming sound going on, this was the German artillery bombarding our trenches, the dull noise was deafening in the dug-out, he probably had wind of the impending attack and was making it as difficult as possible for us. At 5.35 a.m. my officer came and told me to get ready as we were going outside, so we got to the top of the dug-out into the trench. Infantrymen were standing against the side with fixed bayonets and smoking the inevitable fags. Occasionally, one would hear the cry "make way for the stretcher bearers" and struggling along the narrow trench would come the stretcher with some mother's son lying in agony on it. We went along the trench slowly, as one couldn't walk fast, owing to the numbers of soldiers and the muddy surface. As it was still very dark, we had to see as best we could from the sickly glare of the Verey Lights that were being sent up in the air. During our walk from the dugout, I had been allowing my reel of wire to play out according to my orders and as we were walking along I was placing it in a convenient way as best I could. I knew from the very start that as far as communication wires went, enamel wire was useless, because it would be trampled by the men's feet as soon as being laid, but orders are orders, so I carried on. We reached our appointed place and waited for the inevitable Zero Hour (six o'clock). The German bombardment previously mentioned had ceased and all was practically silent, only an occasional shell flurry here and there, a few blurts of a machine gun or an occasional rifle shot. The silence was uncanny. One could hear the Tommy's speaking to each other in hushed undertones. It was that sort of stillness that makes one expect something, hence to have their senses on the alert. A few minutes of this deathlike stillness and then "swash" "bang" "swash" "bang" "zip" "zip" "crash" "crash" "crash", the war and explosions of bursting shells was deafening, This was an unusual 5.45pm bombardment opening out, Mr. Fritz was then retaliating but where they were dropping I couldn't say, as we were all taking advantage of whatever availed itself in the trench side. After about ten minutes or so of this racket, Infantry officers came marching along the trench saying as they passed "Get ready boys, only a few minutes to go". There was a tightening of belts; a few sighs and we were ready. Then that fateful order that sent many a good man to his death. "Over you go boys and the best of luck". Up onto the step and over the top they went including my officer and I. We were both close to the infantry officer who was in charge of this particular company. My little reel of wire was reeling itself out on every step I took. Shells were bursting all over the place, hand grenades were falling, shrapnel from the shells and machine gun bullets went hissing past one's ears, making you duck for all you were worth. The smell and taste of powder from the shells made you cough and gasp, but still we walked on. Dawn was breaking now and it was possible to see more clearly. One could see men throwing up their hands and dropping down dead or badly wounded. Several of the men in my immediate vicinity got it pretty bad, how I was missed, I can't say. Germans were coming out of their dugouts with a sickly paleness on their faces with their hands above their heads signalling that they surrendered. One of our soldiers would be hastily told to see them to our rear, then there were Germans in their dugouts who wouldn't come out, but one soldier would stand at the entrance of the dugout and fling a half dozen of mills bombs. After they had made themselves known to the Germans, they came up from the dugout to find a few British bayonets waiting for them. These were only a few of the sights that I am able to impress on my memory. When our barrage was lifted several times to allow our soldiers to advance and with the Germans being practically taken by surprise, there wasn't much use for my officer and myself, so we stopped and sat down for a rest. I went on a souvenir hunt in the dugouts and obtained a lovely German officer's peacetime sword. It was all inscribed on the handle, blade and scabbard. When I found it, I hid it down my trouser leg. After I had reached my officer again, he asked me to try and get my battery on the phone. I fixed my phone on the wire, but no response, probably the wire was broken into a thousand pieces. We looked back over the ground we had held only an hour previously and what a shambles it was, too awful to describe – bodies of both British and Germans lying around. We looked further to the rear to try to pick up one of my signallers at the battery. He had been told before the attack to be on the lookout for us signalling back, but it was useless. It was just as well that the infantry officer we were attached to didn't need our services. It would have been impossible to signal any messages back to our guns by either wire or flags. After that, we made our way back again, but this time going over the surface of the ground instead of through the muddy trench. We eventually reached our battery tired out, to find all our guns out of range of the enemy as we had retreated that far back from the onslaught of our soldiers and guns. When we got back our first thought was for a good sleep and something to eat, but alas, there was no sleep for us.

All guns were immediately taken out of their gun pits where our gun teams were ready for them and off we went again after Fritz. We travelled over the captured ground through Beaumont Hamel[38] and what a sight greeted our eyes. The road we were going along (if you could call it a road) was nothing but a broken track. Great holes were everywhere making it practically impossible to get along. They had been caused by our heavy guns during the attack and it gave us a good idea of the work they had been doing to assist our men. Dead horses and men were lying all along the road where they had been caught by our shellfire as they were trying to get away. There was an awful stench hovering about everywhere from the dead bodies and the gas from our gas shells. This was barely twelve hours after the attack and even after such a short period our Labour Corps were busy making the roadway somewhat passable by filling the gaping holes and haul-

38 Beaumont Hamel was the sight of one of the most bitter struggles in the Battle of the Somme only being captured in September 1916 3 months after the first shot was fired there on 1 July.

ing the dead bodies of men and horses onto the side of the roadway, where they waited a favourable time for burial.

What George has been describing was his involvement in the Battle of the Ancre, an operation carried out by the 5th Army to increase the Somme salient. It was a last gasp effort by the British Army to produce a better outcome of the Battle of the Somme, which had received so much criticism at home on account of the terrible casualties since 1st July. It was to be the last phase of the campaign. The battle commenced on 14th November 1916 and the purpose was to capture the villages of Serre, Beaumont Hamel, Beaucourt and St Pierre Divion. The objective of the 63rd (Royal Naval Division) was the village and station at Beaucourt. All objectives except the sinister village of Serre were taken. The successes gained were attributed to the "creeping barrage" whereby artillery fired on their objectives according to a time table as the infantry move forward. George's experience with the advancing infantry with his reel of wire illustrates very vividly the difficulty of communication between the artillery and infantry on which so much depended. In those days there was no wireless or radio forward of Army HQs. The Ancre battle was a very significant battle for the Naval division; they achieved all their objectives with great gallantry although at great cost. The Division lost 100 officers and 1600 men killed and 60 officers and 2377 men wounded. The Commanding Officer of the Hood battalion Lt Col Freyburg won a Victoria Cross for his "personality, valour and utter contempt for danger". After the battle the division was withdrawn for two months. However the Divisional Artillery was re assigned to other Corps engaged in the Arras battle.

Guns and ammunition were always the first consideration. We eventually reached the arranged position for our guns. This was a field off the road on a slope of a hill. The guns were placed in line and left without any covering. We were told to make the best of it for the night, the time was about 5.30 p.m. and being winter it was getting dark. Well, being as there were no billets, barns or stables, or old houses for us to go into, we had to make the best of it. The first thing a Tommy does in this predicament is to scrounge around and look to see what he could find among the ruins that were nearly always near at hand. When he saw anything suitable to make a shelter, he immediately set about making his bed for the night. Five other signallers and I went on the hunt for material to make our telephone pit and at the same time our shelter for the night, or, for as long as we stayed there. We found three sheets of German corrugated iron and a bunch of German sandbags; this was sufficient for our needs, so we started to make our little home. First, we dug a six foot square and four foot deep hole filled the sandbags with earth from it and placed these around the edges at about six sandbags high. We then placed the iron sheets over these and on top. We put four rows of filled bags. Having left room for a doorway, we fixed our telephone up, put a blanket at the door to guard against gas and all was ready, except for a comfortable fire. The wood was plentiful amongst the ruins, so we got a petrol tin, put holes in it and lit a fire. Having a few tallow candles we soon had a nice comfy little snug shelter. After an hour or so, we put our blankets down and went to bed. One chap was left at the phones and the others including myself went to sleep. We didn't sleep long though; I woke up with a start to find everybody struggling to get out. When I tried to get out, I found I couldn't even sit up. It was pitch dark with a cold biting wind, which was very much to my discomfort. At a loss to understand what was wrong, I groped for my tunic to get a match and when I made a light, I found what was wrong. The shelter had caved in on three sides, bringing the roof down. After a lot of cursing and laughing, we all stayed where we were and went back to sleep. Daylight broke and we were quickly up and about. We were told we were moving away again. What had happened to our little shelter was easy to understand. Having a severe winter, the ground was frozen hard, we had filled our sandbags with this frozen earth, and we built the walls of our shelter. We had a good stick fire burning inside for a long time, with the result that the heat had thawed the frozen earth and made the roof sag and eventually caved the sides in. We moved away from this spot without even firing a shell. As we proceeded further over the captured ground, we were struck at the awful appearance of the surrounding fields and villages. There was not a whole wall left standing in the villages we passed and the fields were full of large and small shell holes, caused by our and the Germans' guns. The roads were clad with our troops, with guns and various forms of transport all making after Fritz; everybody was in high spirits at the idea of chasing a defeated enemy as we thought.

We eventually pulled up at the village of Miramont,[39] which lay on the banks of the river Ancre, pronounced "ONK". We got our guns into position at once and everybody who was at liberty started to make their billets from material we had obtained from the various smashed up houses. Some were making themselves fairly comfortable in the cellars. One of the most awful sights I ever witnessed occurred at this place. It is necessary to mention in connection with this event, that all our water for drinking and cooking purposes was drawn from the river. It was fast flowing and as such, was fairly clean and pure. One chap was going over to the river for water, when he passed over a piece of open ground, he had just got halfway over this clear space, when without a moment's warning, overcame one of Fritz's high velocity shells, and dropped right in front of him. All we could see for a second or so was a great mass of black smoke. I and several others dashed over to the spot. When we got there, the smoke had cleared away, but the sight which met us was sickening. The poor fellow was lying there absolutely mangled into mincemeat, not a vestige of legs or arms, just a mass of red and black flesh. This man's body was picked up with a spade, just like anyone would shovel refuse in the street. An officer put his remains into a hastily made grave and the short funeral service was read, such is war. It seemed curious to us at night when we were talking about the occurrence in our billets that the shell that

39 Just beyond Beaucourt, the divisional objective in the recent battle. The War Diary reports the Brigade reached there on 9 March 1917.

killed the chap was the only one to fall that day in our vicinity. We all came to the same conclusion, namely fate!

The next day, I proceeded up to some high ground about a mile in front of our guns, with one of our officers. As we set off and as I was walking along, I was letting out telephone wire from a reel I had with me. This wire was a different kind to the one I used when I went over the top of the Somme. It was stronger and covered with insulation. I asked the officer where we were going and he said we were going to try and observe the new German line or trenches and range our six guns on them. This new German Line was commonly known as the Hindenburg Line which gave such obstinate resistance to our men in the latter part of the Somme advances. We travelled on through small clumps of trees for cover and eventually arrived at the foot of the hill. We didn't know exactly where the German lines were and couldn't see a soul in the vicinity; we came out into the open and proceeded up the slope. We were about one hundred yards from the skyline of the hill (the nearest spot from where we could see over the other side of the hill was termed "Skyline"), when there was a "Zip", "Zip", "Zip", three rifle bullets in quick succession. The two of us went down flat to the ground and lay still. The officer said, "There's someone on top of the hill potting at us". He put up his glasses to try and see where the firing came from and his movement brought the bullets once more. This time there were about a dozen and we saw where they dropped far too close to be healthy for us. "By Christ he knows where we are" blurted my officer. "Not half" I answered. We tried several times to get down the hill again, but the quick fire of a rifle answered every movement we made. Several times the bullets came dangerously close. My officer, seeing it might cost one of us our lives, resolved to stay there until dark before any more attempts to get down to the bottom. "Fix your phone up Elder", he said and even this slight task brought two more bullets. We hardly dare move after that. I got the phone, put on the wire I had laid out whilst coming and as soon as I touched it, I had an immediate reply from our battery that was about half a mile away, as the crow flies. "The battery's on now Sir", I said. My officer took the hand piece and said, "Hello battery, get the O.C. quick". "Ah, is that you Sir. Well Sir, there's a German sniper at the top of this hill he has us in line and we daren't move. Can you let off an H.E. or so?" "Well Brown, I might drop them on you instead, how would you like that? Ha, Ha, Ha." replied the O.C., "No Brown, it's far too risky for you because we haven't got the bearings for the guns yet. I am afraid you'll have to stay there until dark before you venture to come away. Don't forget to keep me informed about your sniper, Ha, Ha, Ha, Goodbye Brown". This was the conversation that transpired between the two officers. I was able to hear them both because I had the earpiece of my phone on my head. The time was about 10.00am and we had to lie there like fools until about 4.30pm in the afternoon before we could get away. We arrived back at the Battery like two whipped dogs. Everyone who knew about it was kidding us for all they were worth. During that night, a message came through to my phone from HQ addressed to our O.C. The message was that the Germans had retreated and our scouts couldn't find them; our battery had to stand fast.

We remained here for about three days doing nothing but clean ourselves and our clothes. Early one morning, all was packed up and off we went on the road once again, but this time back over the identical roads we had come along to chase Fritz. Again we passed through Beaumont-Hamel, on our way back and also Englebelmer and Arhau.[40]

40 Possibly Acheux

Chapter 4

Oppy Wood 1917

On 20th March 1917 the Brigade was moved from 63rd Royal Naval Division to become an Army Artillery Brigade which meant it became a sort of 'rent a brigade' in 5th Army. It found itself attached to several different Divisions and Corps for the rest of the war. This may sound very confusing for all concerned but it probably had no effect on George and it is notable that he doesn't mention this re-organisation. It would however have been pretty frustrating for the CO of the brigade having so many different masters. For most of April and May the Brigade was attached to X111 Corps and found itself in the Oppy Wood area. The fortifications there were very well built not by the British but by the Germans in 1915 as indeed they were on the Somme which the New Armies discovered to their cost. Oppy wood was behind the German lines until after the Somme. So for once the British were able to enjoy the luxury of secure fortifications.

After about two days on the road, we went into action at a spot in the vicinity of Oppy Wood[41], which was on the Hindenburg Line. This place was rather pretty to look at; no desolation of war was

41 Oppy is well forward of Arras and has a wood to its west.

notable as in other parts, in particular the Somme district. The fields were beginning to show their green patterns of grass in places and the bushes were sprouting. The ground was of a hard chalky nature, which was a welcome change indeed to the thick, slimy mud of the Somme. We were billeted in some captured German gun pits, of which there were several. These pits were six in number and very elaborately constructed. They were made of concrete about four feet thick and underneath them were passages connecting each pit together. There were rooms attached to each pit for the Germans to stay in. These passages and rooms were about thirty feet below the surface. Some of them led away from the gun pits for about one hundred yards before they came on a level with the surface. The purpose of these was to bring ammunition and stores to the gun pits under cover free from the observation of our aeroplanes. This was in very marked contrast to our own methods. All our gun pits were only the gun itself covered with wire netting, through which was inserted different coloured strips of cloth to give it the appearance of being part of the field or ground where it was placed. There was a raised railway embankment in the valley with Oppy wood in the distance. Our guns were placed behind the railway embankment on our side covered with the usual camouflage, because there wasn't sufficient cover at the guns. The men sheltered at the German pits because there was one very good feature attached to being here, namely that they could be used as a point of observation for our O.C. He was able to observe the German trenches through his glasses with complete ease. On one occasion he was sitting observing the German lines with me sitting below him with my telephone ready to transmit any orders he may give to the guns. Lying in front of me and well within my reach was a large field artillery telescope that was used to see further to the German rear. My O.C. was looking through his binoculars and without taking them from his eyes, he asked me to get the Adjutant on the phone. I rang up the brigade and got the Adjutant. Being curious, I placed my eye to the telescope and what I saw was a wide road away to the German rear and a batch of German infantry. They were close together and seemed to be making for the same direction. I knew it must be this that my O.C. had been watching. Having the ear piece of the phone strapped to my head, this is the conversation I heard between my O.C. and the Adjutant "Hello Brown, Largen[42] speaking," my O.C. said, "Well, Largen, what can I do for you?" the Adjutant replied. "I have got a very good target for our counter battery if you can get them for me." "All right Largen, just hang on and I'll get the heavies for you" the Adjutant replied as he left the phone; in about two ticks someone spoke. "Hello Major, this is the officer of the heavies speaking". Then my O.C. said, "I am sorry to trouble you, but I have such a good target I don't want to miss it. I can't reach it myself, so I want your assistance if you don't mind. I want you to put about a dozen shells on (a map reference meaning the roadway previously mentioned) as quick as possible." "Alright Major, just look out for them" replied the officer of the 8 inch Howitzer Battery and at that I immediately put the telescope to my eyes once more and my O.C. had the binoculars to his eyes. Just as I got settled looking through the telescope, I heard the sound of six heavy shells going over our heads. On the road behind the German lines was the batch of German infantry still passing along. All I could see of the roadway was great billows of black and white smoke. I knew then where those six heavy shells were going. They had dropped dead on the road where the soldiers were marching along. This was repeated about twelve times at intervals of about thirty seconds. When the smoke did clear away, I couldn't see anything on the road. In all probability, the German infantry had been blown to pieces. During this, I heard my O.C. say out loud "My God, My God, this is terrible". He then got down and spoke to the officer of the heavy battery saying, "Thank you, and goodbye".

On another occasion we were sitting in exactly the same spot, my O.C. was sitting and smoking and occasionally looking through

42 Captain WG Largen commanded A Battery from Aug 1916.

binoculars. Mr Fritz was shelling in the valley with nasty big shells, which we knew to be his big 5.9's[43]. They were dropping a good distance away from us so we considered ourselves quite safe. About half a dozen of these 5.9's dropped a little closer on the railway embankment and splinters went sizzling over us. The embankment was about eighty yards away, so even then we didn't worry. All of a sudden without warning, a shell struck the concrete end of the German gun pit where my O.C. was leaning with me sitting beside his legs. There was an ear splitting explosion with clouds of dust and pieces of concrete. I immediately fell flat into a little trench just below; I was none the worse, only covered with dust. After the dust had cleared away, I got up to see how my O.C. was. I fully expected to see him lying mangled, as he had been that close to where the shell struck, but when I saw him, he was sitting in the very spot he had been all the time. He was just dusting his tunic with his hands and wasn't even scathed. I said to myself "By Christ, you're a cool un". These sort of qualities shown by an officer had the effect of making the ordinary rank and file have absolute confidence in their superiors.

Another incident which illustrates the little difficulties that beset us during our everyday tasks concerns the commodity used every day and very seldom considered with the importance it deserves, namely water. The usual methods employed by battery and artillery and in fact infantry, was to have a water cart brought so far up to the trench or gun positions to have the water put into petrol tins and manhandled to wherever it was requested. Other times, the petrol tins were already filled when they came up to the trenches or gun positions. This particular part of the country was badly served with roads; the only use was for horse traffic. Mr. Fritz knew this and consequently took action to prevent us getting our water up. His methods were to open fire with high velocity guns onto the road at very irregular intervals, just after dusk. He would drop about a dozen

43 The 5.9" referred to in many British war time reports are the German medium Field Howitzers which fired a shell of 85lbs a distance of from 6,000-8,500 yards.

shells in quick succession on different parts of the road at different times. To illustrate this better, at about 5.00pm he would drop his first lot of shells, then again at 5.05pm and 5.10pm, then 5.30pm and perhaps no more until about 6.00pm, leaving an interval of half an hour, thus any traffic that had been on the road at 5.00pm and which had necessarily halted when Mr. Fritz had started shelling, got the impression that Fritz would only be shelling at fairly long intervals, namely every half an hour or so. Thereby they would consider they had ample time to get over the part of roadway that was being shelled before Fritz sent any more shells over. But alas, Mr. Fritz would start again perhaps a few minutes after 6.00pm just as the traffic started to move on. Slaughter of men and horses was the result as this had been going on for some time. We lost very many horses, men and transport wagons. The battery O.C. considered it was too dangerous to have carts or wagons sent up this way with water and took steps to ensure an ample supply for the men who were now at the other side of the railway embankment.

There was or had been a pretty large farmstead, only the ruins were remaining. In the yard of the farm there was a well, which is quite a common fixture of homes and farms in France and Belgium. This well had small winders to lower and raise a bucket; it was under full observation of Fritz. Anyone who dared to go to the well in daylight didn't live to bring back the water; therefore supplies were obtained during darkness. Two signallers and myself went to fill six petrol cans of water one night, but when we got to the archway leading through the railway embankment we heard Fritz shelling in the vicinity of the well. We stopped where we were for the time being. Whilst waiting for Fritz to stop shelling, four infantrymen came with petrol cans for water. "Is he bumping the well"? They asked, "Yes", we replied "for about twenty minutes now". "Come on" one of them said to his pals, we'll get further on to the well, he can't keep up shelling much longer, and then they proceeded through the archway and were lost to our view. They hadn't been gone more than three minutes, when the shelling stopped, so we made a move towards them. We groped through the archway to the other side of the embankment in absolute darkness, save for the sickly glimmer of the Verey Lights in the distant trenches. On emerging, Mr. Fritz started again so we chopped flat to the ground to escape any splinters that might come our way. Then finding that we were very much in the open, we took steps to find better cover. The only possible and nearest cover was the brick ruins of the outer buildings of the farm, so we ran to them as best we could in the darkness. Mr. Fritz was dropping shells pretty frequently now all round the vicinity of the well, so we crouched behind a broken wall. We could hear quite distinctly the splinters of the shells spattering against the other side of the wall. We had been in this position for about twenty minutes or so and were rather anxious about whether to stay until he stopped or make a bolt for it. We heard a sound and decided to stay where we were. The sound we heard was of a battery salvo of 5.9 shells. It is a fearful nerve-racking sound in the air, once you hear it, you never forget. We could judge by the closeness of the bombing that they would drop near to us, so we crouched even lower to the ground. They dropped with a thundering explosion and about a second or so after they dropped, one of the others and I looked through a hole in the wall and in the momentary glaze of the exploding shells we saw the dim outline of the four infantrymen and the windlass of the well. We then bolted back over as fast as we could in the darkness and made our way back to the dugouts without getting a drop of water. It was early next morning that our other two signallers went to get water and were back to the dugouts again with three tins each within half an hour. Whereby it had taken myself and four others about two hours to get to the vicinity of the well and back again with empty tins. One of the chaps, who had been for water, remarked quite casually that there were two infantrymen lying dead at the well. Such was the price to be paid for ordinary water. During our stay in this spot, this well was indirectly the means of many a man being severely wounded or killed.

One evening about 6.00pm I was doing my turn of duty on the telephones when I received a call from brigade HQ for our O.C. as I had the earpieces of the phone on my head, I was able to get knowledge of the conversation. The message that was conveyed over the wire from our Colonel to my O.C. was that our people had information of the German intention to make a big raid on our trenches at 8.00pm prompt that same evening. Our O.C. was instructed to open fire at precisely one minute to eight o'clock on what was called S.O.S. lines. This meant in detail that all our guns would open fire at the time stated and all the shells would drop or burst about six feet above the ground immediately in front of our own front line trenches. It was also arranged that after firing five minutes in that manner, all guns had to increase their range fifty yards and continue until ordered to cease fire. The effect of these arrangements can be easily imagined by any intelligent reader, thus it would be that the Germans would attack at their arranged time and would be caught by our gun fire just before they reached our trenches then finding they were found out they would immediately retreat back towards their own trenches. During their retreat, our guns would put fifty yards on their range and the Germans would run into our shells again whilst endeavouring to regain shelter in their trenches. In view of this important development, precautions and arrangements had to be made immediately. Officers were put on duty at the guns and gunners started to prepare the shells. We had a telephone wire down to the infantry HQ and it ran over the surface of the ground right up to the third of fourth line trenches. As the wire was in a very exposed part and liable to be broken with German shell splinters, it was necessary to have a signaller looking after it whilst the firing was in progress. I was detailed to go on this task by the bombardier in charge of our signalling arrangements. I picked up a telephone, about twelve foot of loose wire and prepared to get out at about 7.40pm. I asked the bombardier for someone to go with me, which was the standing rules, in case one got wounded, there was always the other one to help him and also carry on. After some hesitation on the bombardier's part, I went off on my own. It was a fine night, a bit cold, but otherwise all right. I made my way over the wire allowing the wire to take me; by this I mean that to see the wire on the surface of the ground that was honeycombed with shell holes, was practically impossible, so I had to slip the wire into a loop made by the thumb and forefinger tips joined together to allow it to slide through. As I walked along, I proceeded until I considered I was about halfway between our gun and the trenches. I then stopped and sat down to watch events. I hadn't long to wait, for no sooner had I filled my pipe and lit up, than a miniature hell opened out. I think Fritz's and our guns opened out at about the same time. The explosion on the trenches and the hiss of shells going overhead from our guns are too much to describe accurately. All along the trenches one could see lurid yellow flashes, which were the shells bursting, then up in the air one would see Verey Lights of various colours, which were signals from either side for artillery direction. Altogether it was a beautiful sight, if one is allowed to speak in such a manner. As all this started I connected my phone with the telephone wire, by means of two ordinary safety pins inserted through the wire and then fastened to my phone by a short length of wire. I spoke to my battery straightaway. "Hello Geordie is that you", "Yes" I replied. "We can't get the infantry" the battery said, so I tried to get the infantry on my phone, but got no reply. Therefore it proved that the wire must be broken between the infantry and myself. Off I went struggling along over the broken ground in total darkness, except for the flitting glares from the shell explosions and Verey Lights in the trenches. The shells were going overhead as I was going along with the wire slipping through my hand. Suddenly, I felt the jugged strands of the wire in my hand; I had come to an end. I fixed my phone on again and spoke to the battery telling them I had found the break and would put it right as soon as possible, but the question was – where was the other end? I groped about with my hands on the ground as far as I could without leaving go of the wire, but to no avail. Then I realised that if I let go of the wire to find the other end, I could have all my troubles over again. Therefore, I got a broken trench board, stuck it up on end and fastened the wire to it. Then I went to find the other part. Having a rough idea of the direction that the wire ran, I circled around a few times scraping with my feel and hands, picking wires up now and again and connecting my phone to find out if it was our wire. Eventually, I found it and after speaking to the Infantry, I started to search for the end tied to the trench board. To find the trench board, I lay flat on the ground with my cheek touching the earth and looked along the surface and no matter how dark it seemed, I saw the dim shape of the board sticking up, so I made my way towards it pulling the wire that I held along with me. I was brought to an abrupt halt by the wire refusing to stretch any further, so judging that there must have been a piece blown out of it, I unfastened the twelve yards of wire and joined it. That brought me a bit nearer to the trench board end, but not near enough. There was still about eight or ten yards short so without wasting any more time, I clipped the necessary length, cut off a wire that was lying near and joined up my own. After I had fixed it properly, I connected my phone to check if it was working I then heard the infantry officer giving instructions to our guns saying where he wanted the shells to drop. I was out on the wire all night, mending it here and there sometimes near my battery then towards the trenches backwards and forwards. I was on the go in the dark until I flagged out. The shelling and racket of machine guns in the trenches continued all night and well into the day. It was about 6.30 or 7.00am when I connected my phone and was told to come in. I got back to my battery pretty well tired out and lay down to get some sleep.

About a week or so after, I was sent for by my O.C. I was busy shaving with soap all over my face, so I just rubbed it off and went to see him. He said as soon as I stood in front of him "Oh Elder, I believe you ran out to our Infantry wire the other night". "Yes Sir" I replied. "Alright", the officer then went on, "Well Elder, I must congratulate you upon your work, our Infantry wire just happened to be the only one that was kept in working order during the bombardment, all the other battery wires were broken up, so I am putting through a recommendation for you". "Thank you Sir", I replied and went out. About a week after this interview, I was in front of the O.C. once again." Well, Elder" he said, "I sent a recommendation through to the Colonel and he can't see his way clear to allow it to go any further himself, owing to your previous conduct, but he is fully prepared to give you a full bombardier's stripe back again, if you care to accept it". I stood silent, thoughts flying through my head, I was in a fix whether to accept it or not and I eventually said yes. I was promoted to full paid bombardier taking effect from a fortnight previous to the day of this interview.

My "Previous Conduct", relates to happenings that occurred at a place called Bully Grenay, which was the scene of our first entry into action on our arrival in France. I was then NCO (Non Commissioned Officer) in charge of the battery signallers; consequently, I had about sixteen signallers under my charge. Being NCO in charge, it was my duty to go every evening to draw the rum issue for all my signallers and this issue amounted to about a pint and a half of neat rum. One particular night, I had drawn the rum and when I brought it to our signal dugout I started to share it out to all who were present. I was immediately greeted with cries of "I don't want any Geordie, nor me"," same here", etc, with the result that there was about nine tenths of the rum left after one or two had had a nip. There was one chap on duty at the phones who didn't take any rum, so four others and I who were off duty had it between us. We boiled some water and obtained some sugar from our emergency rations and made a good toddy. We were all sitting on the wire beds laughing, joking and nipping at the toddy and eventually the rum proved to be the strongest. We had dropped off to sleep under the influence. I was awakened by someone tugging at my arm, trying to haul me out of my bed. When I was fully aroused, I saw the Orderly Officer, a sergeant and a signaller sitting at the little table with the phones. I asked the sergeant what was wrong and the officer replied "Elder you are under close arrest" and out they went. They hadn't been gone half an hour when in came an NCO from the guns to take charge of me. I did no further duty for about four days. I was just walking about wherever I chose in company with the NCO who was responsible for my safety. On the fifth day, I was paraded in front of my O.C's billets with the sergeant major and escort, then marched into a room, in which sat the colonel and my O.C. The sergeant major's remarks were "Prisoner and escort attention, right turn, quick march, halt, cap off". I was standing right in front of the colonel's chair. "You are charged with being drunk and neglect of duty, whilst in charge of battery communications on active service". Then followed a lecture on how NCOs should show an example to the men and he finished with this question, "Prisoner, will you be tried by me, or a Field Court Martial?" I knew full well his sentence would be nothing compared to what a Field Court Martial could inflict. I said "I'll be tried by you Sir", so after he took all the evidence against me, but none from me, he passed the following sentence "Prisoner, you are reduced to the permanent rank of a gunner". The sergeant major went on "Prisoner and escort about turn, quick march, left turn, halt, prisoner cap on." All the Battery was standing outside watching, then the sergeant major took out his pocket knife, opened a blade and held the sleeve of my tunic and cut the stitching away sufficiently for him to get hold of the stripes with his finger and thumb. Then with a quick tug and they came off, likewise the same procedure with the other arm. After this was completed, he said once again "Prisoner and escort, Shun, dismiss" and it was over. I was now a gunner in rank with my pay reduced from 3/2½d to 1/2½d per day. All my pals rushed over to shake my hand saying I was better without the stripes and everybody was pleased. It transpired that on the night of my arrest, the Orderly Officer and sergeant were checking the battery to see that everything was O.K. At about 11.30pm they came into my signal dugout and found everybody asleep. On the table was a message that the chap on duty at the phones had taken before the officer's visit. Naturally, the chap at the phone had been woken up first and had told them where I was lying. When they woke me up I was a little groggy from the effects of the rum I drank earlier. The message that had been taken had only one word, namely "Cabbage"; in the code translation this meant gunfire on a particular part of the trenches by our guns. Therefore, because the chap on duty at the phones left the message lying on the table instead of delivering it to an officer or showing it to me, he had committed a crime and made it worse by going off to sleep whilst on duty. To sum up the whole affair, I had been punished for another crime, simply because I was in charge and strictly speaking, the only crime I had been guilty of was being asleep under the influence of rum, although not actually on duty. The foregoing story is "my previous conduct" referred to by the Colonel some four months after the occurrence. On its account, he couldn't pass my recommendation further to those higher in authority, but because I was promoted to full bombardier, automatically squashed my previous offence, according to army regulations.

As I have previously mentioned, there was another set of German Gun Pits used as billets for some of the men and adjoining these pits was a German dugout. This was exactly sixty two steps from the surface to the floor of the dugout. Each step was about a foot in depth, making a total depth of approximately sixty two feet. There were two entrances each about twenty yards apart and at the bottom of each stairway there was a passage about six feet high and four feet wide. This passage led from the foot of one stairway to the foot of the other. In the centre it was considerably wider, about double the width of the stairway. Inside the passage, it was pitch dark even if the sun was shining outside and if any German shells were dropped above the dugout all one could hear down the passage was a dull thud, so it was quite safe in the dugout if there was any heavy shelling going on. This dugout was used as sleeping quarters for myself and two signallers. One particular night about 10.00pm the three of us had finished duty for that day and were in the dugout preparing our beds ready for a good night's sleep. One of my pals thought he would have some supper in the shape of Quaker oats. He started to make a fire in a petrol tin. The wood he had was twigs and pieces hacked off the sides of the passage with an Infantry bayonet. Having used some of his letters for papers he put a match to it, it flared up but didn't burn properly and after a good deal of puffing and blowing, the fire refused to burn. Another chap and I were just about gassed with the smoke from the fire. We then remembered about a large tin cask that was in the corner of the passage we pushed in the lid, and found it contained a thick liquid just like oil. Thinking it was some German gun oil we put it on the fire to make it burn. We put about a cupful of this so called oil onto the fire which was just smouldering, it leapt into a lovely flame and we were as happy as larks, on went the tin with the Quaker oats and we had visions of some supper. When the fire died down on went more oil. This operation had been repeated about a dozen times when one of my pals said he was going outside for some fresh air, then went towards the stairway. We looked after him as he staggered along the passage. Thinking there was something wrong with him, me and the chap who was making the oats got to our feet to follow him. Oh what a shock I had, as soon as I stood on my feet, I went as dizzy as could be. My chum was groping along the passage in a similar state. My head was thumping something terrible as I made for the stairway. We struggled upstairs, our throats burning, we could hardly breathe. I was in front of my pal and the other chap was already outside, I had just reached the top and taken a few deep breaths of fresh air when I heard a crash and moans down the stairway. The two of us who were outside marched down as quickly as we could where we found the other chap lying head down, with his feet wedged in the stairway. The moans from him were awful, we thought that either his back or neck must be broken, what a great struggle we had to get him to the top of the stairs. When we were eventually all on top, we could do nothing except lie on our backs staring up to the stars. God only knows what that liquid was. When the smoke had cleared away sufficiently, we all went down the dugout again. Our first task was to bring out the cask with the so called oil and dump it into a shell hole and then go to bed. A little while after this incident, I was making my way across the intervening ground between our signal dugout and the dugout previously mentioned, I had just finished my duty on the phones and was going to bed in the dugout, I was by myself because my two pals were on duty. It was a lovely night, the moon and stars were all shining. Lovely Mr. Fritz was putting some 5.9 shells around and about the guns, but far enough away from me to cause any worry. I made my way across in my own time, picking my path between shell holes. Having reached the right hand entrance or stairway to our dugout, I struck a match and went down slowly; I had reached about halfway down when there was an awful crash and explosion in the entrance. I was hurled down to the bottom as lumps of wood and earth came hurtling down after me. Choking with dust and half buried with debris I struggled in the dense darkness to free myself. After a good deal of panting and exertion, I freed myself and got into the passageway. Strangely, after falling downstairs and amid all the earth, I still retained my box of Blue Cross matches in my hand. I lit the candle we always had ready. I then felt and looked myself all over to see if I was damaged, then made my bed and got into it and was soon asleep.

The next morning I got up early to go on duty again. I made it my business to see what the cause of the smash was the previous night. The conclusion I arrived at was, just as I had reached halfway down the stairs, one of Fritz's shells had dropped right into the entrance. All I could see of the entrance from outside was a hole about two feet square but before the shell had dropped, it was a neat entrance about six feet square. The stairway was blocked with earth and planks of wood. When I examined the mess at the bottom of the stairs, I wondered how I had got out without so much as a scratch, if I had only been a few seconds later I would have got the shell in my back.

A day or so after, I was standing at one of our gun pits talking to the gunners, it was a fine sunny day at about 11.00am. Alongside the pits there was a foot worn path, which was eventually used by our infantrymen when going to the trenches. This particular morning, we saw two of our infantrymen walking down the path; they were talking together just as any pals would do. They had their full kit on with their rifles slung over their right shoulders. Just as they approached our guns, a couple of Fritz's 5.9 shells dropped at their feet. We all dashed over to them as fast as we could. We got to them before the smoke had cleared away, they were lying where they fell, one chap was dead and the other was moaning. I stooped over him to see if I could do something, but he never answered my questions, his eyes were rolling all over and it was curtains for him a few seconds later. We looked to see where they were hit and saw they had low body wounds, one chap had the lower part of his abdomen shot clean away. We put their bodies into the side of the ditch and reported the matter to the nearest first aid post by telephone. They were eventually moved to have a respectful burial.

Chapter 5

Arras 1917

On 9 April the Battle of Arras was launched in a gale of sleet to hold the Germans and prevent them from attacking the French Armies to the South who were in some trouble having recently sustained serious mutinies. As frequently was the case the battle started well. The Canadian Corps took Vimy Ridge, a remarkable feat of arms which not only secured a vital piece of high ground which had hitherto overlooked the Allied Armies but also struck a mighty blow for Canadian nationalism and is today a shrine to the Canadian Army. 3rd Army under General Allenby made good progress east of Arras and of particular note was the well orchestrated artillery barrage in which a new 106 fuse was used for the first time. It was designed to burst when it grazed barbed wire. Even so the battle did not achieve the break through so often dreamt of. Instead the battle continued until 17 May with little to show for it. The result of the Battle of Arras was an advance of 7,000 yards but at a cost of 160,000 casualties. 315 Battery would have played their part in the artillery battle and no doubt George would have known all about the 106 fuse but he could hardly have mentioned this in his diary. 315 Brigade began the battle supporting XVII Corps of 3rd Army who attacked south of Vimy. By

13 April they had transferred to XIII Corps who were brought forward from the Reserve to attack. 315 Brigade was supporting 2 Division and 63 Royal Naval Division, their old friends who were in action beside them.

We packed up and pulled out our guns to proceed back away from the trenches. This was done in darkness so we got out without any casualties. We were very lucky in this respect as the roads were noted for casualties at night. After a few days travelling, we went into action in front of Vimy Ridge. When we were in position and all our guns were continually firing, we were sick of the noise and sleep was out of the question. At last the artillery pounding came to a climax.

One morning at 4.30am our infantry went over the top an hour before dawn. I was again up in our trenches with one of our officers for observation purposes and for artillery direction in conjunction with the infantry. The weather was very cold and the kilted troops who took part in the attack felt the cold much more. I was sincerely sorry for them when I saw them shivering in the muddy trenches waiting to go over the top, as some of them were blue with cold. When I went forward with the infantry, I didn't have any wire or telephone with me as I had at Beaumont Hamel on the Somme. My equipment for signalling consisted this time of a French electric signalling lamp. This was made up in the form of a harness, which was made of leather shaped for the shoulders with a belt to go around the waist with a large leather disc and a metal slot to place on my breast. These were riveted together and were part of our routine like putting on a coat. Fastened to the straps at the back of the harness, were eight leather pockets, each with an electric dry cell with wires attached, these were slotted along the shoulder strap and eventually fastened to the metal slot on the disc on the breast. The lamp fitted tightly into this metal disc and the four electric bulbs it was fitted with went into the electric cells on to the back of the harness. On the back of the lamp was a small switch to enable the wearer to turn the light on and off. Another lamp was placed at our observation post, which was about halfway between our guns and the trenches. The orders were for each lamp to look for the other when flashing at an arranged time on the morning of an attack, to establish communication between each other, the message could then be sent to the guns by Morse Code. The officer and I were up in the trenches at about 3.00am. The infantry were all busy preparing for the assault, they were opening boxes of cartridges and Mills hand grenades then shared them out to carry. Others were standing leaning against the trench sides smoking the inevitable fag. At approximately 4.20am our artillery bombardment opened up. A marked peculiarity of this bombardment was on the second it opened up all would be deathly still and quiet. A stillness that seemed to be unreal and not of this world. Then suddenly, four sixty-pounder guns firing in quick succession, thus "Pom, Pom, Pom, Pom", rudely broke that stillness. These guns had a peculiar sharp, clean, crisp crack when they were fired. Then just as these cracks were ringing in your ears, all the guns on that particular front would start belching out shells, in the shape of eighteen pounders about fifteen or twenty shells a minute, then all the atmosphere was filled with deafening reports. One had to shout if the person you were speaking to was standing at your elbow. When this bombardment started, it was pitch dark and when the first lot of shells dropped upon the German ranks, I never saw such a display of fireworks in all my life; the sight was magnificent to witness. As far as the eye could see there were yellow and red flares of bursting shells. Up in the air were rockets of different colours, red, blue, green, groups of two red and one green, three reds and three green, yellow and red. All these colours and groups of colours had three different meanings to either side that sent them up, the sight was wonderful to behold. By this time the German artillery were doing their share of shelling and their shells were mainly directed into No Man's Land, on the front line trenches. In this particular attack our front line, second and third were deserted and quite empty. Our attacking troops were in readiness further back awaiting the order to go over. They were also waiting to let our artillery do the work of smashing Fritz's barbed wire entanglement and to kill as many Germans as possible. Then at 4.30am, which was zero hour, our guns lengthened their range and over went the infantry. My officer and I also went over and we kept falling into shell holes, which, by the smell of powder that greeted one's nostrils, we knew to be just newly made. We struggled to keep alongside the infantry officer we were attached to, shells were dropping all around and the noise was awful. A glance to either side would reveal in the glare of lights and bursting shells, men falling, other times shrieks of pain would greet your ears, then the sharp crackle of machine guns and rifles. We carried on at walking pace up to the stoop of the hill towards the ridge that Vimy Ridge was part of, the whole district was reeking with smoke from the shells, both German and our bodies were lying all over. The light of morning came and we were able to see where to walk. German prisoners were coming towards us in groups of twenty or so, with two Germans carrying our wounded on stretchers. The whole ground was churned up by shell-fire. When dawn had fully arrived, we reached the top of the ridge to see the bursts of our shells in the far distance with the infantry well advanced. The infantry officers had left us some time previously and we were "on our Todd[44]". My officer halted and asked me to try and signal back to our battery observation post. I turned around and started flashing my lamp. We thought we saw an answering flash, but were not sure and after trying for about half an hour or so we gave it up and started to return to our battery. On our way back, we saw the grim toll of war, our soldiers were lying all over in all sort of positions, just as they had fallen, some had smiles on their faces, and others had agony pictured in their expression, while some had no faces, having been practically blown off. Some were sitting down just as if having a rest and when I looked at one chap I couldn't find a mark on him to show where he had been shot, but on closer examination with my officer, we raised his tin hat and just underneath the fringe of his hair was a small hole showing he had been shot clean through the head.

44 On your Todd is an old fashioned expression meaning being on your own.

These sights were enough to make anyone sick, but one had to buck up and guard against it. As we got further to the rear, we met battalions of infantry making towards the front to relieve their comrades who had made the attack. Guns and Infantry transport with supplies of ammunition and rations were all making forward as quick as possible. We eventually reached our guns to find every one of them out of range, with all the gunners black with smoke. The normal maximum range of an eighteen pounder gun is 6,500 yards, but our guns on this occasion had finished up firing at the wonderful range of 11,500 yards[45]. To get this extra 5,000 yard range with the gun, the tail had to be lowered into a hole in the ground, which had been previously dug by the gunners at the finish of firing. Each gun was in great danger of turning a somersault as each shell was fired. Our guns remained where they were for about two days or so.

During this time the battery fitter attended to any minor repairs that were necessary to the guns on the spot. Practically all the six guns had new recoil springs put into the buffers. We then pulled out the guns and off we went on the road once again. We went forward after Fritz for nearly eight miles. The roads we travelled on were still littered with refuse of war, namely dead horses and broken wagons that were mostly German. We halted to allow the stores to have a place fixed for them and to arrange a wagon line. When this was completed, the guns went forward to pick a position for firing again. It was a very dark night and it was only by the aid of the officer's electric torches that the drivers of the gun teams were able to pick their way over the treacherous ground. As usual, Mr. Fritz was doing his regular night shelling and owing to the dense darkness, it was difficult to get an idea where they were dropping. We were struggling over ground that was littered with shell holes three parts full of water. One gun after another would get stuck in the mud and the horses were unable to move them. The cry would go up "Gunners, Gunners", and they had to hurry to the gun in trouble, get around the wheels and assist

45 The official maximum range was 11,100 yards

the horses to pull the gun out. This was happening roughly every ten minutes or so, one particular gun was so badly sunk in the mud that it was impossible to get out. We were all tugging at ropes, some at the spokes of the wheels, the horses were kicking and flinging as they were being lashed with the whip, but to no avail. Then, without a moment's warning, down came one of Fritz's 5.9 shells right alongside the gun. We all scattered some distance off in the darkness, but the cries and shrieks of agony brought us back. There were no fewer than six wounded. When we got them sorted out with the less serious ones sent away to the dressing station, we were able to attend to the one who was doing the most shouting and crying. Some of the men had been attending to him as best they could from the start. When I went to him I found that it was our officer who had been supervising after getting the gun out. A stretcher was brought for him as he was very badly wounded in the small of the back and the bandages were useless. He kept shouting and struggling and several times he fell off the stretcher, it was impossible for us to keep him still. His hands face and clothes were thick with wet mud through falling off the stretcher; the agony he was in was pitiful to witness. When he was eventually handed over to the RAMC at the Aid Post, he turned very quiet. The doctor just looked at him and shook his head, he must have known because the officer just shouted once more and then went out. His name was Lt. Bennell[46], a finer officer one couldn't wish to meet. This particular gun the officer had been endeavouring to get out the mud was so firmly embedded, it had to be left until daylight before it was possible to get it away and only then by the aid of twelve horses and men. The ground in this vicinity was churned up so much; it was practically impossible to fix up the guns in a firing position. All these circumstances, although providing heart-rending tasks to both gunners and horses, also gave ample testimony to the fierce destructive shellfire of our guns.

46 Lieutenant Donald Bruce Bennell joined the Army in 1903 and was commissioned in the field in 1915. He was killed on 16 April 1917 and is buried in the Roclincourt Valley cemetery just NE of Arras, he was aged 31 years.

We stayed in this locality for about two days and were then withdrawn without even firing another shell. We travelled a couple of miles behind the Front Line to a point further south. The position our guns took up was about half a mile in front of the ruins of Thiepval[47] village. This village lay in a valley and was plainly visible from our guns which stood on the crest of the hill in front. Our front line lay about a hundred yards from the other side of the ruins and as our guns were very close and would have been easily seen by the Germans if we had fired in daylight, we had strict orders not to fire, coupled with as little movement as possible during daytime. The weather conditions were very severe at this time, the cold was intense, the shell holes were full of solid ice and the ground was treacherous to walk on. When it had been in its soft mushy state, it was very uneven owing to the numerous shell holes and gun wheel ruts etc., so one can imagine the state when very severe frosts set in. All these wheel ruts, trucks and even holes made by men's feet were frozen like stones and to walk over this sort of ground in darkness was very dangerous indeed. There were several cases of broken and sprained ankles in our battery caused by the ground alone. Our rations at this time were also very meagre; breakfast consisted of one dog biscuit and a strip of fat side bacon about the length of one's forefinger and it was a rare occurrence to have a solid unbroken biscuit. When one went for the breakfast ration, the cook used to use his cupped hands as a scoop and dip them into a biscuit tin that had once been neatly packed with whole ones, but were then all broken into little scraps caused by travelling over uneven roads. Then, when one obtained these scraps of biscuits the cook would cry in sarcastic humour, "Hoy, want any dips", just imagine having bacon dip with broken dog biscuits that were as hard as the ground. The tea we had was about half a pint and by the time one got to his dugout, it was cold as the weather. Dinner consisted of what was called Bully Stew, this was made by putting about three or four small tins of Fray Bentos Bully Beef and one tin

47 A key position during the Battle of the Somme.

of Pork & Beans with about twenty potatoes into an army Dixie, then bringing it to a boil. Each Dixie had individual rations or was shared out to twenty-five men, so one can imagine the nourishing dinners we used to have. Tea was a repetition of breakfast without the bacon, which was replaced with a little cheese or jam. Those who had cheese couldn't have jam and vice versa. If you wanted jam for a change, you had to put it onto an envelope, or any piece of paper, as it was impossible to have it spread over scraps of dog biscuits. More often than not, men had it thrust into their hand straight off the spoon or a piece of stick it was dished out with.

The dugouts were roughly made during the night in darkness, the one I had was about six foot square and four foot high from floor to ceiling. The roof was about two foot below the level of the ground and when one was getting in, they had to practically sit down on the step or what formed it, then drag oneself or slide in. When inside one had to keep continually in a stoop or always sit down. We had a little fireplace fixed up but the difficulty was how to get wood to burn, as one did need a fire when in the cold weather. There were no hedges or trees and the old dugouts that contained the wooden planks couldn't be approached during daylight because of being seen, at night, it was also very difficult. One night a party of four of us, resolved to go to one of these dugouts to get a plank or two. We set out at about midnight without an axe or chopper, but we knew what we were going to use to get these planks that formed the stairway of the old dugout. Having arrived at the entrance after a lot of struggling and hard knocks from falling on the uneven ground, we felt our way down the stairway in the darkness. Rats scampered away beneath our feet, lovely big ones like cats. When we reached the bottom, which was about thirty stairs down, we ventured to strike a match and light a candle (this was always handy). With the light we soon got what we had gone for, a box of Mills Bombs which had been left by the former occupants. We came up to the surface after blowing out the candle and opened the box very, very carefully, as Mills Bombs are very dangerous to tamper with, the four of us then got one in each hand and took the metal pin out. We approached the entrance of the dug-out once more and stood in line and at the word "Go", let fly with both bombs down the stairway. We then hopped away about twenty yards to so, as quickly as possible. Eight bombs went down that stairway in the space of a few seconds and the roar the explosion caused was like a big tank bursting. We waited about fifteen minutes and then came back to the entrance. We saw that several planks were leaning across the stairway being partly dislodged by the explosion, but what made us look more earnestly was a glare at the bottom of the stairs, which enabled us to see the dislodged planks. One of my chums was about to venture down the stairs, when "Boom, boom, boom" reached our ears and clouds of smoke came from the stairway. These explosions were going off intermittently we therefore came to the conclusion that the first eight bombs we had thrown down had ignited other bombs that must have been lying on the floor. There was no doubt that there must be a fire at the bottom of the dugout caused by the exploding bombs and realising this, we thought that desertion was the better part of valour and we decided to "Hook it". We left leaving the fire in the dugout to our esteemed friends the "rats". On our way back to our dugout, we remembered about a dump that lay just to the right of our guns, so we decided to see if we could get some firewood or anything to burn. This "so called" dump was a great mass of material used in the trenches. It consisted of wooden trench boards, coils of barbed wire, sandbags, iron stakes, shovels, rifle cartridges, Mills Bombs etc. At these dumps, there was always a guard with rifle and fixed bayonet and if he caught anyone tampering with anything he wouldn't hesitate to use them. Well, we passed behind our guns and approached the dumps, having noticed where the trench boards were lying by their light yellow colour showing up in the darkness. We decided to go past them singly at intervals and endeavour to snatch one of the piles if possible. Two of my chums went to look for a trench board, until I was left alone so I followed them. On approaching the dump, I observed the guard walking around so I waited until he got round the far side, then I hurried up to the trench boards, picked one up onto my shoulders. They are not lightweight, being about six foot long and two foot wide. While I was staggering across the frozen shell holes the best I could, my nerves were all on edge, all manner of thoughts passed through my head. I imagined the guard seeing the light coloured trench board moving in the darkness and challenging me, but lucky for us, we got away. I met my three pals about a hundred yards further on, who were resting and waiting for me. Each had a trench board so we were sure of a fire at last. We picked up our burden and proceeded to pick our way towards the direction of our dugout, as we thought. Suddenly, we were startled nearly out of our skins by the cry in the night of "Ready one, two, three, four, five, six" and then a deathly pause, which was followed by the command "Fire". Someone who seemed to be just in front of us spoke these words. We realised to our concern that we must have walked right in front of our guns, all in the space of a few seconds. We dropped our trench boards and fell flat upon the ground before the command "Fire!" was uttered. Then the ear splitting reports from the six guns, and the sudden swish of the six shells passing over us. We got away as fast as our feet could go over the ground in the darkness. What a sense of relief we felt when we again heard the order "Fire!" right behind us. We dared not think what might have happened if we hadn't got down on the ground quick enough. Eventually, we reached our dugout, lit a fire, but alas as was usually the case, one comfort can bring discomfort. We were all sitting around the fire congratulating ourselves on having obtained a supply of wood, then off would come tunics and shirts and the hunting began. It didn't take a magnifying glass to find what we were looking for. No mercy was the order of the next half an hour or so, even after the massacre of a few hundred; we had to go out into the cold air to obtain a little relief from the irritating itching. The majority of men in the battery had no boots and those who had them couldn't put them on, on account of skinned heels caused by the bad fitting Jack Boots that we all had while in the Somme district. Those men who had no boots nearly all had trench waders, which were a large rubber boot coming right up to the thighs. They were splendid for wet Weather, but alas during this awful cold we were experiencing at this particular time, these gumboots were useless. Our feet were never warm so to walk over the frozen ground was next to torture. When one arose from his bed in the morning, he had to put his warm feet into these cold Gum Boots which always had a thin coat of ice inside, being the moisture from his limbs left inside from the night before. On top of all these discomforts, I had several boils on the back of my neck, two on my hips and also a slight touch of dysentery. Night after night I had to crawl in and out of our little dugout to go to the latrine, which was just a hole in the ground with a canvas screen around. I would get nicely settled into my bed with my blankets curled around me and be dozing off to sleep, when I would have to get up to go outside. I was never more sick of life than at this time, what with insufficient food, no water (only for tea and breakfast and then only half a pint), boils and dysentery and the severe cold, it made one feel like doing away with oneself. The dysentery went as it came, but the boils were another story.

About this time, we had an extra ration issued, a slice of bread along with the scraps of dog biscuits for breakfast. Instead of eating the bread as I was sorely tempted to do, I obtained a little ice and melted it over a fire, brought it to the boil and soaked my bread and formed poultices to apply to the boils on my neck and hips. I carried on this treatment for about three weeks until I got rid of them, though not thoroughly, as I still retain the little hard knots on my neck to this day. One may wonder why I didn't go to our doctor with these troubles, I could have easily done so, but at the same time as I fully realised the benefit I would get by doing so, I also realised what would happen to me. The doctor would have immediately sent me away to hospital, which would have meant comfort, good food, bed and skilled attention, but on the other hand I would have been sent to some strange battery when I was well again and this was the last thing I wished for. I couldn't think for one moment of leaving the lads I had been with all my days in the army, this and only this caused me to endure the suffering and discomfort.

The cold was awful for another month or so and it was a great pleasure for us when we heard we were going out of the line to have a rest and be refitted. Eventually, we pulled out our guns in the middle of the night without much trouble or casualties. We marched for some considerable distance along the frozen roads and although we all had to walk, we bore the discomfort to our feet, thinking of the rest we were going to get, as well as the relief to our ears from the continual shellfire. We travelled north, all the time stopping at nights in any field that would accommodate all the battery, horses, guns, ammunition and baggage wagons. Whilst travelling along the roads we kept noticing to our dismay that our observation balloons and Fritz's were always in our sight and seemed quite near to us as we went along. This fact coupled with other unmistakable signs, led us to believe that the "Rest Tale" was all "bunkum", and this later proved to be the truth. We stayed in a field overnight and the next morning all guns and gunners were ordered to be ready at 1.00am. The ammunition wagons etc., remained where they were, the guns proceeded up towards the line of observation balloons, which in other words meant the Line or "Action". About mid-day, we reached the front, in-between Vimy Ridge and Mount St. Eloi. This part of the country was very well wooded, having not been devastated by shellfire. It was broad daylight when we pulled our guns into the pits which were already there. The dugouts were large, plentiful, and comfortable having been previously made by our troops. We went through the usual routine, fixing our wires up to different headquarters, infantry included. Next morning it was sunny but awfully cold. Our O.C. went up to the trenches to register his guns on Fritz's front line. I went along and curiously enough, although we had to walk for about an hour and a half, we never saw a single shell burst. We reached our first trenches and the O.C. had all his six guns on firing with me passing his orders down the wires of my phone. Having got all his guns to drop their shells where he wanted them, we returned back to the battery. The firing of the guns was the only firing whilst we were in the pits. We stayed at that place for about a month, during this time the weather improved considerably. This, along with decent grub and opportunities to get a good "All over bath", we weren't long in pulling ourselves together again. Another main factor to our well being was the complete absence of Fritz's shells. This in itself was the biggest help, as there was nothing more destructive to the mind and nerves than his continual shelling, especially at night.

All "little bits of heaven" must come to an end and this one did, to our sorrow. After the orders came to move, we were not long in getting out on the march again. No doubt, we had had a long needed beneficial rest and the march we were on showed the benefits in more ways than one among the rank and file. While going along the roads they were singing the old favourites "Tipperary etc.," altogether the men were quite jolly. The weather was now becoming more summer-like, although it was only about the middle of February 1917. It was a welcome change trekking along the roads. From the signs we saw, civilians etc., we knew that we must be going some considerable distance away from the real locality of the War, namely guns and trenches. There were several rather humorous incidents during our journeys along these roads to our unknown destination, no one knew where we were bound, not even our officers. The procedure was thus, the whole brigade would be marching along the road in what is termed 'Column of Route', this means that the brigade must march together in the following order, first the headquarters' staff with the colonel leading, secondly came the first, second, third, Howitzer Battery and lastly the ammunition column. Then one would observe a dispatch rider on a motorcycle coming along to meet us. He would stop and hand the adjutant a message, who in turn would hand it to the colonel. The motorcyclist then went back the way he came and was soon out of sight. Where he came from no one knew, but they did know he came from the High Command. The message he delivered to our colonel was the orders for that day, namely where he had to take his brigade to and where to stay the night. The higher command's intentions regarding troops on the march were kept secret up to the last possible moment. This happened every day whilst we were on the march, which amounted to four days. One of the humorous incidents that happened during this march was as follows, we were slowly passing through a good-sized French town and as was always the case, whenever a shop was seen there was a rush for it by the gunners and even drivers who allowed their horses to follow the gun or wagon that happened to be in front. The particular shop was a "Boulangerie", which means a "Bake House" where the people took their bread to be baked. About a dozen of us entered to buy some bread and after a good deal of "Pow Wow" one chap obtained two large cakes of bread. When he got them into his hands, he turned about and dashed out the shop without paying, the majority of the men and all but a corporal treated this as a joke, but another chap and I gave chase. The woman behind the counter was screaming blue murder and the corporal tried to pacify her without any luck. We kept looking out of the doorway to see how far away the battery was, as we were anxious not to be left behind, but we also wanted some bread. The corporal made another attempt to get some bread and was successful. He received three or four cakes and tendered a new French 20 Franc note for payment. When he checked his change he found the woman had taken pay for the two cakes that had been stolen, but try as we could, we couldn't get her to give it back, so we had to leave her to her own opinion regarding English troops, we then ran about a quarter of a mile before we caught up with the battery.

Haig had long favoured an offensive in Flanders and he now found himself in a strong position to do so. The BEF was nearly half a million strong and now well provisioned with shells and other stores of war. By May 1917 Haig was beginning to form his ideas of a two phased attack from Ypres, the first extending as far as Passchendaele and the second out as far as Thorout which would be supported by an amphibious landing near Ostend. Operations on the Arras front were therefore scaled down and the emphasis shifted to the Ypres Sector. There were to be two attacks in the first phase towards Passchendaele, the first was aimed at the Messines Ridge and the other a few weeks later directed at the Passchendaele Ridge. This would explain the move of 315 Brigade to the Ypres Sector at this time and which George has just described. In July the Brigade moved from 5th Army to 2nd Army which was commanded by Sir Herbert Plumer and their task was to take the Messines Ridge. This operation was perhaps one of the most meticulously planned operations of the War and was successful. George's brigade and battery were supporting the three Corps of the Army IX,X and the II ANZAC Corps and as the operation proceeded it moved from one division to another as and where the artillery concentration was required.

We eventually passed over the French and Belgium Frontier into a large city called Bailleul. We stayed on the outskirts for a couple of days. During our stay we were paid and allowed to go into the city. This opportunity wasn't to be missed, so everyone who could go did. Another eight men and I went into the city the first night we were there. We made a round of the entertainment and eating-houses having a right royal time and I don't think any of us slept that night with our boots off. The second night, my pal and I went back to the city and had our photos taken at an established photographer[48]. After this, we proceeded up the main street towards the market square, when suddenly there was a rush of air, a crash and a loud explosion right in the centre. Paving stones were hurled in all directions, some crashing through shop windows, others hitting passing horses and all in the space of a few seconds. Everyone in that square was scampering away into buildings and doorways, up side streets, as fast as their legs could carry them. My pal and I went into a shop and waited, then another

48 This is no doubt the occasion when George's photograph which is illustrated was taken. Perhaps the other photo in possession of the family is of Bombardier Watmough in whose memory this book is dedicated.

two shells followed the first in quick succession, dropping into practically the same place. The wisdom of getting quickly out of the way was amply illustrated as these shells were fired by the Germans by a very large range gun. We were told that it was a daily occurrence in the city reminding us once again of the task we were engaged in.

The next day we were on the move once again, but this time in single batteries. We left the city of Bailleul and on our way, we observed ordinary directional signposts with "TO YPRES 20 KILOMETRES"; we were enlightened as to which front we were going. We travelled past the usual undeniable signs such as ammunition dumps etc. Darkness was well established when we pulled into a field, the blue glaze of gun flashes were plainly seen on the horizon and the Verey Lights could also be seen. These lights seemed to be right around for three parts of a circle, practically the shape of a horseshoe and was called YPRES SALIENT. We tied our horses to the horse lines and had our little bivouacs placed to our advantage. It was not long before we were settled down into our blankets, pretty well flagged out after considerable marching, but sleep was not for us that night. We were suddenly awakened by blasts from whistles and cries of "Put that bloody light out". These whistles and cries were reported time after time, we all knew the reason why, it was the German bombing aeroplanes. On looking out of our little tent, my pal and I saw the sky light up with one range of searchlight flashes, then the sound of the aeroplane engines. The moon was shining bright, but no planes were seen, but they could be heard, "Crash, crash, crash", these explosions were repeated time after time. One could see the dull red flashes in the far distance and as each succeeding series of crashes and explosions came to one's ears, we obtained a fair idea of where they were dropping and the direction the German bombers were making for. Then suddenly a number of other men shouted "Look, there they are passing the moon" and sure enough in looking in the direction of the moon, we could see one plane after another passing the moon's light and then fading into the surrounding darkness. Although out of sight, the throb of their engines was coming more loud and clear with the crashes of the bombs also getting nearer; this made us a little anxious. Our horses that were tied to ropes were fidgeting and stamping about as if sensing danger and they weren't far wrong either. Without a moments warning, "Crash, crash, crash", then a slight pause and again "Crash, crash, crash". Six bombs dropped into the field adjourning ours with thunderous explosions, the like we had never heard before and the whole ground shook. The anti aircraft guns got some of the bombers in the searchlights and were thundering away their shells at them, thus adding to the noise, which was deafening. The planes then seemed to turn about and come back again.

Next morning we saw the damage done in the field next to ours. There had been nearly sixty heavy draught horses tied to ropes belonging to the ASC[49] when the six bombs dropping amongst them. The sight was indescribable, great pools of blood were lying on the ground, just like pools of water after heavy rain, horse's legs and heads in different places, bodies ripped open as if with some gigantic knife, the sight was sickening to witness. We dared not imagine what would have happened if they had dropped amongst us.

Two others and I went to a cinema which was originally a barn, the roof was completely blown off during the periods of shell fire, the four walls were still standing and to make a roof, a large tarpaulin was put over and fastened. We were in this cinema looking at the pictures when overhead came the German bombers again; the films were kept on during the bombing. The whole place shook with the explosions and the next morning, we were amazed to see where some of them had dropped. No less than six great bombs had dropped within a hundred yards of the cinema. About three days after this we had marching orders for guns and gunners to proceed up the line. At 5.30pm we set off to go into action at YPRES, which was to prove the most awful nerve racking experience of the whole war.

49 Army Service Corps who were responsible for transport and supplies.

[50]In nearly all Belgian and French farmyards, houses etc., there were wells of various depths. The people drew all water supplies for household purposes from these. Naturally, when we soldiers were billeted in these barns and cattle sheds, we used to get our water from the wells, although forbidden to some extent by the military authorities. All water had to be chlorinated or disinfected before being used by the troops, but we used to use this water for mainly washing purposes and at times for individual cooking uses. This particular farmer in question was busy cleaning his cow shed, when a number of our men, myself included, were going to the well with canvas buckets for water to wash with. He immediately flew into a rage when he saw us, he was "jabbering" away in his own tongue at us all the time. He wheeled a barrow load of cows' filth to the well and tipped the whole load down into the water; the words of the troops are unprintable.

Our gun positions in this part were in a valley in "Ypres Salient" a very dangerous place. A small gauge light railway ran through the valley for the purpose of conveying military supplies, to both Infantry and Artillery. Underneath these railway foundations were our gun pits, each of the six pits were made pretty strong with bulks of timber, corrugated-iron with stones and earth. Water was continually oozing through the ground at the bottom of the gun pits. This just caused us to obtain hand pumps to keep the water down to a comfortable level. At the left hand of the gun pits, there were the ruins of a large white house, named the White Chateau. It had been a lovely building at one time. Whilst standing behind the guns looking to the front, rear and each side, it was possible to see the familiar observation balloons of both German and English. At night the position was more than confusing because we were absolutely surrounded by "Verey Lights". These lights were rockets that were sent up from both German and British trenches as soon as darkness set in. On examination of these conditions in detail, it was easy to see that the shape of the extending trenches were exactly the shape of a horseshoe. The position of

50 George notes that this was May 22nd 1917

our guns at this time was inside the horse shoe at the toe. This as we later learned to our sorrow, put us in an unenviable position of being shelled by German guns from front, right and left.

In company of a few signallers, we had a look around the locality, it was nice and quiet. We came to a large lake, called Zillibecke. The surface was actually about six foot above the level of the surrounding country. It being a fine warm day and with baths not a regular custom among troops, we took the chance of having a swim and wash at the same time and it didn't take us long to strip off into a natural costume. We were soon romping about in the lake, swimming all over and thoroughly enjoying this unaccustomed luxury. But without a minute's warning, we heard the familiar gurgle of the German 5.9 shells and with a shriek and a crash, into the middle of the lake crashed two shells and we all felt the vibration of the water. Oh, what a dash for the side of the lake. I think we must have broken all speed records. Out of the water we scrambled, snatching our clothes into our arms. We ran as fast as our legs could carry us to some cover behind a large mound of earth and put our clothes on; of course we then started to laugh. This was just a slight illustration of the complete observation the gunners had of the surrounding country.

At about 8.30am on May 30th I was instructed by our Major to get a telephone and wire and proceed with him to the trenches. We made our way in front of our guns and went along to Zillibecke Lake to the far end before we entered the trenches proper. As I have mentioned previously, we were in a valley and consequently low-lying ground. The trenches were consequently very shallow, about 3 feet deep, we were not able to get deeper because of water oozing up. These particular trenches kept this depth for a considerable distance until the rising ground of the hillside had made it possible for them to be deeper but only about 5 feet. Mr. Fritz was fully aware of this and used to take every advantage of such conditions. We had entered the shallow trenches and were hurrying along as fast as the zigzag route of the trench would allow. It seemed rather amusing to me at first to see ourselves walking along a trench, the top of which was only up to our knees. The amusing thoughts were suddenly banished from my mind by a sudden deluge of shells called "Pip Squeaks" dropping behind us in the part of the trench we had just passed along. We hurried faster and kept looking back to see where they were dropping and dropping they were, like rain. One would eventually think that they were following us along the trench and every minute we were fully expecting them to overtake us in our stride. The strain of these thoughts was awful, still on we went, not another soul in sight. The ground was rising and the trench was a little deeper as we went on, but to our eyes came a shock that we were not in any way looking for. Shells were dropping well in front of us alongside the trench that we were in. We were practically trapped in the trench between two fires. The Major halted and looked both ways then said "Well, Elder what are we to do?", I replied "Get over the top Sir", "Right, off you go then" he said, I didn't need telling twice. I scrambled over the trench top; the Major wasn't long in following me. We made off at right angles to the bursting shells, which by now were getting closer and closer to each other. We halted about fifty yards away then watched and waited. Eventually, the two sets of bursting shells met and kept raining down on one spot in the trench for about five minutes, then ceased and so proved to us that our timely halt and consideration of the situation saved us from certain death. We learnt later that this particular trench was a very dangerous one, it being continually shelled by Fritz in irregular bursts of severe intensity. After he stopped shelling, we made it back to the trench again and entered at a different point to where we had left, and then proceeded to the third Line or reserve trenches occupied by our Infantry. The Major, after a good deal of searching around various communication trenches, found a suitable firm footing, so was able to get a good view of the part of Fritz's trenches that his guns had been responsible for. After he had taken various readings from his map and compass bearings on given spots, he decided to return without firing his Battery. My heart was in my mouth when I saw he was going back along the trench which we had come through. All went well until about half way back, we seemed fated to endure more shellfire from Fritz. This time they were 5.9 shells, considerably larger and more destructive. Over they came, two at a time into the vicinity of the trench we had just traversed and as before, he was creeping along the trench route with each successive "two shells". We both hurried and ran, keeping a respectable distance between the shells and ourselves. The most comforting fact about this affair was that Fritz was sending two shells over about every thirty seconds and increasing the range about twenty five yards each time. We eventually arrived back at the Battery none the worse for our journey, apart from rather strained nerves and a practical education of gunnery from Fritz's point of view.

One day we all got some pay. The NCO received about fifty Francs and the others twenty five. Money was practically useless where we were, there being no canteens in our vicinity, so we signallers got ourselves together one night and talked the matter over as to where and how we could obtain some rations or eatables by buying them ourselves. After various suggestions, we came to the decision that another signaller and I should go to Albert early next morning to obtain what each of us wanted. The next morning at about 8.00am, we set out without asking permission from our officers. We had three hundred Francs in our possession, which were donations from each signaller; the sum in English money was about £11. One can imagine what our orders were "Spend the Bloody lot Geordie" was the parting salute that we received on setting out. Albert was about eight miles away from our battery and had to be walked with gumboots on and over uneven roads. On we went trudging along, our feet were giving us some trouble but we stuck at it, thinking of what we would get with the money. After being lost a few times we arrived at Albert, at about one o'clock, it had taken us five hours to walk eight miles. We had a look around the city first, not having had the opportunity before and one sight that gripped us was the figure of the Virgin Mary with baby

Jesus in her arms. The statue was hanging from the spire of a church without any visible means of support. The superstition among the troops and civilians who lived in Albert was that when this statue fell, the war would be over. Well, it didn't fall[51]; it was blown off by one of Fritz's shells some time after our visit. We eventually found a British expeditionary force canteen in the centre of Albert and proceeded to obtain whatever we could get. These large canteens were stocked like a grocer's shop. What we bought are too numerous to mention here, but a selection are, spice loaf, Nestles milk, tinned fruit, Quaker oats, tinned sausage, tinned rabbit, biscuits, sweetbreads, cocoa and camp coffee. We each had five sandbags to carry. On our way back we went into a French house and had a feed of fried eggs and chips and a bottle of Vin Blanc. It took us nearly eight hours to walk back with our loads and what a reception we got when we returned to our signal dugout. While we had been away, they had obtained four petrol tins of water so the Quaker oats were soon cooked with Nestles Milk poured over, then the tinned fruit followed, pears, apples and pineapple and to finish came the rum ration.

About 9:00am on June 1st 1917. I was ordered to take a phone and wire and meet one of our officers. Off we went to the trenches. We travelled over the same trench as on May 30th and curiously enough all was quite still. Not a shell from Fritz came to within five hundred yards of us. We reached the observation post that the Major had fixed on May 30th and the officer had a good look around. He decided this place wasn't quite suitable for the work he had to do. We left this spot and went further up the trenches, eventually into the front line, all the way along, particularly at the turns or where two trenches met or crossed, I noticed boards fixed to the soil on the trench side. The reading on these boards were varied, such as "Beware of Sniper", "Keep your head down", "Don't pass along this trench in daytime", these were warnings to troops drawing their attention to each particular

51 It DID fall in March 1918 when the German Offensive reached the area just east of Amiens.

spot. Naturally, they were very much respected. At the front line there were various saps[52] running out into "No man's land" for about 20 yards or so. These saps were trenches with no outlet in "No Man's Land". My officer went into one of these saps and cautiously peered over the top as far as safety would allow. Natural curiosity prompted me to follow suit. The scene that greeted my "one eye," was one of utter desolation, shell holes all over, stumps of trees, wire in heaps, just looking like large bundles of dirty straw, thrown into a raggy mass. Our approximate distance from Fritz's front line was 30 yards. Because of the fine sunny morning we were easily able to see the masses of black tangled wire fitted to the front line trench. We didn't look long at this scene on account of Fritz seeing our movements. Often, Artillery Officers and Signallers had been doing similar work in the front lines and didn't take the necessary care, with the result that Fritz saw movement in these front line trenches and immediately pounded the place with shells and trench mortars. Our Infantry didn't like to see Artillery men doing this sort of observation as they knew what it generally led to, so accordingly we took great care not to be seen. My officer told me to fix my wire to an Infantry exchange and get the Battery on, and I wasn't long in carrying it out. My officer having had one gun drop a high explosive shell among the German wire, immediately ordered gunfire. Over came our shells shrieking as they sped past us like a hurricane to crush into the German wire. Shell after shell went among the wire until after about five minutes, the officer ordered a ceasefire. He told me to get my wire in quickly in case Fritz started shelling in return. Whilst doing this, I had a look over the top at the wire our guns had been firing at. There were great bare gaps where it had been blown away. I wasn't long in getting everything ready and on our way back we came along a different trench, from which we had a lovely view of the city of Ypres. Every road was clearly outlined to one's view in the brilliant sunshine. We

52 A sap is a narrow trench, normally for communication, made by digging at an angle from the existing trench.

arrived back safely at about dinner time and I was ready for my bully stew and pork and beans.

The following day I proceeded up to the trenches with the major to help get the barrage fire arranged for his battery. Having reached the desired spot in the trench where we had both previously been, I fixed my wire and telephone up to the Infantry line and was soon in communication with our guns. The Major was looking through his binoculars at the German trenches. "Battery, eyes front", I was told to send to the battery, then followed his next order "No.1 gun angle of sight 10 min elevation, 20 degrees more right range 2,500 H.E. Report when ready". After a few seconds came "No. 1 gun ready Sir", then the Major said "Fire" which I repeated over the phone. Over our heads shrieked the shell with a terrible hiss and rushing noise. From where I was sitting I could see the trenches by raising myself up slightly. This I immediately did to observe the shell when it dropped. I saw the burnt and thick clouds of black smoke when it dropped past Fritz's front line. Immediately the smoke had cleared away the major said H.E. 2,450. The shell came over and dropped nearer Fritz's front line, H.E. 2,400 fire was ordered. Once more a shell shrieked to burst right into Fritz's front line, this was the major's desired object. The next order was "No.1 gun cease fire" Then after the major had worked out one or two positions on his map and made a few notes, he ordered me to repeat to the battery. "All guns parallel lines on No. 1 gun H.E. report when ready". Battery ready wasn't long in coming to my ears. "Fire" was the Major's order, I wasn't missing this, so up I got as far as possible to see them drop along Fritz's front line for about forty yards, there was one mass of black smoke where the shells had dropped This was repeated about six times at intervals of about 30 seconds, cease fire was ordered and I was told to get my wire in. We made our way back again to the battery without incident.

On the following Sunday we woke up to see dreary, dismal, damp weather and curiously our thoughts and moods were quite contrary to the weather, because Sundays seemed to be a special day that Fritz made efforts to distribute his iron rations amongst our batteries, namely shells. Due to the weather, observation was very difficult, so we knew that there wouldn't be much shelling done by Fritz or ourselves on this occasion, hence our elated feelings. The day wore on without incident, only an occasional shell dropping now and then without giving anybody any reason to worry. Dinner and tea came and went. We sat about in groups around the guns talking and enjoying the fresh air as best we could. Soon after tea, dusk seemed to set in rather early and then darkness followed enveloping everything in a damp blackness, this in itself made one's flesh creep. An unearthly stillness seemed to hover all over, never a shell burst to be heard. In our dugout amongst the telephones, one could always be interested in doing something. There were always some message to take etc., but this night the telephone was like a deaf mute not a sound came through, which made it necessary for me to test it now and again to see if my wires were in good condition. The whole district seemed to be stricken with an unearthly stillness. My signallers sat about the dugout in quietness, the usual carry on with mouth organ or cards absent, there seemed to be an atmosphere of foreboding hanging around and the candles burned steadily without a flicker of flame. Nerves, nerves, nerves, made of steel, couldn't stand it; each and every one seemed to be straining their ears to listen to sounds that weren't to be heard. Some short time after 8.00pm, several signallers laid themselves down and others were dozing where they sat. The little wood fire that had been burning merrily in the petrol tin died down to red and white mushy embers. Listen, "Sh" yes it was "Crash", right behind the guns dropped an 8 inch, the stillness was broken at last. "Crash, crash, crash", one after another in quick time they dropped, our candles couldn't be kept alight now. Shells dropped, the concussion caused the corrugated roof on our dugout to lift a few inches and crash back again with a lot of dust and earth, making us cough and curse. Soon there was nothing to be heard but bursting shells, it just seemed that Fritz intended to blow us to pieces and had been quiet all day in preparation. The shells seemed to burst right in the entrance of the dugout, judging by the results inside. We were in complete darkness, only the glowing ends of the fags were to be seen, then the telephone started to buzz "Hello is that you Elder" said our major from the dugout, "Yes, Sir" I replied, "Everyone alright there?" asked the major, "Quite alright Sir" I said, he then said "Keep your ear to the phone, if it gets any worse, we will have to clear out". "Very good Sir" I replied. I told my signallers what he had said, "Worse?", they repeated, "If it gets worse than this, God help us". We soon noticed that Fritz was sending gas shells over by their familiar thud when they landed, we used to hear these thuds in-between the crashes of the 5.9's and 8 inchers. This was Fritz's method of disguising them to take troops by surprise with the gas. Naturally, we all pulled out our gas masks ready for protection if need be. By this time, the shells seemed to be dropping faster than ever. Nothing but crash, crash, crash could be heard, something terrible to listen to in darkness, then the telephone buzzer started to buzz rather lustily. I immediately answered to find the Major speaking "Hello, Elder" he said, "Inform all No.1's to clear out with their detachments and take their No.7 dial sights[53] with them. Also clear out yourself with your signallers, "Very good Sir" I replied. I then made my way to the entrance of our dugout to go and give the Major's instructions. On my way, I informed my signallers what the Major had said. Before I got to the gas blankets hanging in the doorway, two of the signallers said to me "Here Geordie, we are going to hook it now, so we will tell the No.1's (Sergeants of the guns) as we go past". "Right O" I replied," it will save me the trouble", so out they went. As they moved the blankets to get out in rushed the gas-laden air from outside. In the darkness we soon smelt

53 The No 7 Dial Sight was introduced for field artillery in 1910. The dial sight on the gun itself was designed so that guns of a battery were parallel in their zero line. This was usually done using a director probably the No 3 Director, but alternatively guns could be given an angle to a distant aiming point. When a battery of guns fired it was important they all fired on the same target and direction. A gun without a dial sight would not be able to fire at all accurately. George would have known all about this.

and tasted the pineapple flavour of gas and immediately put our masks on and there we sat knowing that everyone had left the gun positions but ourselves. We tried to light the candles, but the continual crashing and explosions of the shells wouldn't allow it. No sooner would the candles be burning, then shells would come over to put them out. Curiously enough, when gas was about, it was the habit of the men, to gradually ease off the masks to sniff and to see if it was still about, foolish no doubt, but facts are facts. We were doing this, one after another until we found it impossible to take our masks off and breath without coughing. We then started talking to each other about what we should do, stop where we were, or hook like the rest. I told them I was going to get away to safety. We were running the risk of being hit with hundreds of splinters of shells, besides it was possible to be hit direct with a shell. If you were in a dugout, no splinters could touch you and it was only by a shell dropping dead on top of the dugout, that one was in danger and if this did happen, those inside wouldn't know. Three others were in the same mind as me, but others said they would take the first chance they got to get out of it and they did, one after another. When they were darting out between shells dropping, we took care not to let gas in, by fixing up another blanket. The four of us were the only persons on the position; we were sitting in complete darkness with shells bursting all over the vicinity. The roof of our dugout seemed to be alive, as after every explosion of a shell, it would drop and down came showers of dust. We sat for about half an hour after the others had left, talking about them, and wondering if they had been hit or got away. Suddenly without any warning, there was a loud thud right in the entrance of the dugout and a loud hissing noise, which we knew immediately, was a gas shell. Our masks were on in "a jiffy", as we realised what delay would mean. This last incident seemed to put us all in the same frame of mind and although we couldn't speak to each other, we made signs by pulling each other towards the dugout entrance, signifying that each of us meant to get out of it. The four of us went to the entrance and waited until his next salvo of 5.9's dropped. We hadn't long to wait as he was sending them about every two minutes. Over they came and burst about fifty yards away judging by the glare they made. This was our chance to get out. We judged that it would be two minutes before the next lot came, so we went into the darkness holding each other's tunics. We made for the direction of Ypres and walked along as best we could. All around us we could hear gas shells dropping and dared not take our masks off. We struggled along, falling into shell holes half full of slimy water, tripping over pieces of barbed wire, which was sticking out of the ground. The eyeglasses of our masks were becoming hazy with our breath and heat from our faces. Our chins were wet with moisture from our mouths caused by the mouthpiece of the mask, so we were in a very uncomfortable state. Now and again the ground would be lit up by the sickly glare of Verey Lights which were being sent periodically into the air from the trenches. It was by this and this alone that enabled us to struggle along until we reached a light railway, which we knew would take us right into Ypres. Gas shells were still dropping but not many 5.9's. Still keeping our masks on we made progress along the light railway, but we had several shocks on our way. I fell down over something and was horrified to find it was a dead soldier. This was also happening to my pals and we avoided several dead men by going slow. Our nerves were in a very strained state after these incidents. As we got further along the railway line, we had to push our way through crowds of Infantry, who were standing still or sitting on railway bogies. They were all probably waiting until Fritz stopped shelling before they proceeded to the trenches. The Infantry we passed, all had masks on and in the darkness we had a horrible vision of them standing and sitting there like a crowd of demons. Eventually, we reached Ypres in the vicinity of the gas works and moat. Still keeping our masks on we went across the moat to the Infantry dugouts. We entered through a gas blanket and were immediately stopped by a Sentry who also had his mask on. He led us along the passage, past six blankets and handed us over to a sergeant before he left us to go back to his post. Noticing the sergeant had no mask on we ventured to take ours off, when we did, what a relief. Our noses were sore, the spring gripped our chin, our necks were all shaven, and we kept falling down many times and were in an awful mess. An officer asked where we belonged and when we told him, he said it must have been awful up at the batteries. It was 03:30; he said Fritz had been sending gas shells into Ypres since 21:30. When he mentioned the time, we were amazed to think it had taken so long to come such a short distance. In normal conditions, we could walk from our guns to the Infantry dugouts in Ypres in twenty minutes, this time it had taken us from about 23:00 to 03:30, quite a good testimony to the conditions we endured. The officer showed us to some wire beds and gave us blankets, hot tea and bread and butter. After our meal, for which we were very thankful, we each got into bed and were soon off to sleep. We woke up and asked the time from an infantryman, when he said 09.30 we got a shock. We got out of our beds and made our way along the passages to the entrance. We went outside to find the sun shining gloriously. We were soon on the light railway making our way back to our battery. All along the railway track were dead bodies wearing gas masks. Soldiers were busy clearing them away on stretchers. Gas shells were all over the track, great holes everywhere made by 5.9's and 8 inches. The four of us stopped, looked at each other and said "How did we miss all this last night". We soon reached our guns to find everybody back, with us the last to return. I was immediately sent to the major to account for our long absence, when I explained everything to him, he was very good and considerate and said not to stay away so long next time, and so ended one of the most fearful nights I have ever had.

Following the previous awful night's affair, we were rather hoping for a quiet Monday, but we were all disappointed. We no sooner had our breakfast, when Fritz started again similar to Sunday evening. Because it was a fine day, Fritz was able to observe his shooting from his observation balloons that were high up in the air to the right, left and front of our guns. To the naked eye these balloons seemed to be no more distant than a mile or so. Therefore, one can readily understand that persons in the balloon with powerful field binoculars could easily see every movement and shell burst that mattered. These advantages were very much made use of by Fritz and illustrated to us by his accurate artillery shooting. During the hour or so after breakfast, we all had to leave our guns and dugouts no less than three times, owing to his intense shellfire on our position. It was very annoying indeed to have to do this, as in my opinion, we were running considerably more risks by going away and returning than we were by staying, but our Major's orders had to be obeyed. I particularly remember leaving a small piece of bread from my breakfast ration and putting it on a little shelf in our telephone pit, when we were back in our dugout after our third "running away", the bread was like a piece of coal in colour, caused by the smoke and reek of Fritz's shells. Of course it wasn't thrown away, Oh no, I cut all the black parts off and added it to my stew. After we settled down to our usual routine work, only possible through Fritz stopping his mad antics, I was told to get ready to go to the front line trenches with our officer to witness and report on a practice barrage which was going to take place. Off we went and reached our intended place in the trenches, previously arranged between our Major and the 2nd Lieutenant whom I was with. We were in a small sap in our second line trench with a small type of dugout jutting off. In this dugout was a fairly large peephole suitable for observing Fritz's trenches for a very good radius in all directions. It being a nice sunny day, one could see very clearly and make out objects with the naked eye. Having no telephone to restrict me, I was free to look out and see things for myself. My officer was looking at his watch intently; suddenly he said that there were only a few minutes to go. Then suddenly an awful roar of artillery broke the fine sunny morning calm atmosphere. The whole air seemed to be vibrating with the rushing shells; the noise was deafening. When looking over to Fritz's trenches, I was amazed to see the change that had taken place since previously looking at them. The sight that met my eyes was wonderful to see, all along Fritz's front line trench there was a mass of black and white smoke, stabbed at intervals with red and yellow flame, up in the air was a similar curtain of smoke and flame. It just seemed that each shell had an allotted place to slip and burst. Included in this panorama of bursting shells were Fritz's trench lights in series of three's, one red, green and yellow. Similar groups and colours were to be seen higher than the smoke from our shells. These were his SOS lights, signalling them to open fire immediately on our trenches, in view of our possible attack. Altogether, our guns only fired for about five minutes then suddenly ceased. My officer then put up his binoculars which he had been using and made preparation to go back to the battery. He hadn't proceeded for more than a few yards along the trench when Fritz sent over a terrible barrage similar to the one we had just sent him. Crash, crash greeted our ears, smoke and fumes and the stench of shells filled the air. We ran as best we could along the trench until we came to an infantry dugout, which was about sixty steps down to the bottom, then got in for shelter, so we were quite safe when we were down there. Although we were about seventy foot below the surface of the ground, we could distinctly hear the thud, thud of Fritz's shells. Fritz retaliated for about ten minutes. After he stopped, we made our way back along trenches that were smashed in on the sides with shell fire, we reached our battery without further incident and I was personally relieved to be out of those trenches; I was ready for my "Bully Stew" right enough. The afternoon passed uneventfully, but at nearly midnight over came Fritz's gas shells by the hundred. We had to sit with our masks on for a few hours for safety and what a relief it was to be able to take them off and lay down for a few hours rest.

Chapter 6

Battle Of Messines Ridge

The preparations for the attack on the Messines Ridge were meticulous. For once the battle was picked as being particularly well organised and it was preceded by an intricate Artillery plan. General Plumer's 2nd Army received additional artillery units to prepare for the battle and no doubt 315 Brigade was one of those. There were 2266 guns made available for this battle, most of them 18 pounders like George's but 756 of them were medium or heavy artillery pieces. Each 18 pounder was issued with over a 1000 rounds. The preparatory barrage commenced on 26th May and finished on 1st Jun having fired 3 ½ million shells. The actual attack started at 03.10 on 7th June with nineteen mines exploding below the Messines Ridge with a blast so savage that it was heard in London.

On June 7th our guns and all guns on the front open fire at 03:30 and our boys go over the top, I am on duty on the phones. A terrible explosion takes place on Hill 60, blown up by our people. Oh, the noise is deafening and terrible. At 07:00, shrapnel bursts around our guns, also 5.9's and 8in shells and I gave up all hope of ever getting out of it, but "duty is duty, so stick to it George!". Our troops gain all objectives by 13:00, but Fritz has spotted our guns and is trying to blow us out, but not yet. All the guns slow down the rate of fire and eventually stop at 19:00. Fritz has been giving us hell; thank God no one is hit. He is missing our dugout and guns by only feet it is 20:00 – Ah! At last he stops, thank goodness. I want to go to the latrine, so off I go to a shell hole he has just made. All quiet up to midnight, when Fritz starts with sudden bursts at us. Gas and shrapnel at the same time, but we twig it and get our masks on. I now have to send a message to brigade on the buzzer to get our 15-inch turned onto the German guns, who are giving us hell. About ten minutes after 15-inch batteries open fire in the direction where Fritz's shells are coming from. After another fifteen minutes, Fritz stops and it is quiet all night.

Went to O.P. with the Major for the purpose of registering two guns. Observation Post was on top of the Hill 60 mine crater. What a hell of a time we had there. I gave up hopes of getting back, but thank God I did. Major got hit on the fingers. At old position again at 9pm SOS from trenches at 10.30pm, all guns on front immediately open fire. Fritz sends gas shells over to us from 23:00 to 04.30. Oh what a night, it absolutely smashes ones nerves sitting with masks on all the time, but thank goodness we had no casualties.

Very quiet on front, came out of action at 22:00 and galloped like mad through Ypres. Fritz was shelling every road; several old houses were on fire. We arrived at the wagon line at 02:00. Left wagon line for a place called Westoutre[54], a new camping place. Not a bad village, but no time to go there after 19:30. At 19:30, myself and another Gunner are sent up to old Battery gun position that we just left to find one NCO and three men who are missing. We set off on cycles, but darkness and heavy rain overtook us, so we got into an old barn and slept until daylight, then we went up to the line. After a very hot experience going round the outside of Ypres to the old position, we find the men in an old dugout which is nearly blown in. We get them away, but we cannot get back through Ypres for the Hun's shelling,

54 Westoutre is located 11.5 Km south west of Ypres.

so we have to take cover for two hours before we eventually get an opportunity to get away. During our wait a 5.9 bursts in front of me and the gunner, it was just six yards from us when it dropped, Oh, what a narrow shave. Eventually, we arrived at Westoutre at 19:00, exactly 24 hours after leaving. We had nothing to eat or drink all that time, but we did all we wanted and said nowt.

Left Wagon Line at 8am on advance party for battery arrived at Crois de Poperinge on the Belgian & French frontier at 09.30. Went to camp to clean up and clear up generally for battery arriving, fine camp, huts and stables etc.

Fine day, had a good hot bath and a clean change. Fritz comes over in his planes and bombs the city causing a lot of deaths and damage. One of our officers is wounded by them and goes to the hospital.

On July 1st The King arrives at Ballieul,[55] we see him go by in motor, well-guarded planes above, front and behind.

Our artillery opened a heavy barrage on enemy trenches at 04:00. Infantry attacked and are doing well up to now, 11:00. I am warned that I am to go on leave tomorrow; well it takes my breath away. Fritz starts to put shells around our guns, I do feel nervous, I trust to luck and pull through. I leave the guns at 14:00 today for the Wagon Line. Just as I was leaving the battery, Fritz counter attacks and shells back areas; well I had the wind up. Eventually I arrive at the wagon line at 17:00 where I slept for the night.

It was during the latter days of August that I arrived back in France after 10 days' leave at home with my wife and children, for me it was like 10 minutes. I eventually reached my own battery at a spot on the Messines Ridge, which is in front of Ypres City, on the right facing the German lines. We had several different positions during our stay in these parts, always moving the guns at night. At one of these positions, our guns had been ordered to fire about twenty shells per gun at different specified periods during the day. It was during

55 In July George gets a few visits to Bailieul and gets "canned" again. July was a quiet month. He celebrates his 25th Birthday on July 26th

one of these bursts of gunfire that an incident happened, which is worth detailing. One particular gun crew had a chap whose work during the firing was to load the gun with the shells. He was pretty deaf with the continual firing and eventually he was backward in obeying orders, which were shouted to him during the firing. This particular gun was placed directly in front of my telephone dugout, about twenty yards away. I was standing right in my dugout doorway ready to pass orders from the major if necessary and naturally I had a good view of the particular gun; they were firing as fast as they could load and pull the trigger. This particular gunner's name was Bentley. He received a shell to load and in his haste he struck the steel work at the breach of the gun with the shell instead of putting it into the base. Naturally, the shell dropped to the ground at the gunner's feet, no one took much heed of this and went on with firing the other shells. Our officer who was directing the firing was standing near and it was he who noticed the first signs of trouble. He gave a loud shout to the gun crew and pointed to the ground. There sure enough was the shell that Gunner Bentley had missed the base of the gun with. It was hissing and smoking as if on fire; all the gunners saw it when the officer pointed to it, but because Bentley was slightly deaf he hadn't heard him. When I took stock of the scene, all that was in the pit were Gunner Bentley and the smoking shell that could explode at any moment. We were shouting to him to get out; he heard us and turned around with a smile on his face, saw the smoking shell, walked to it, picked it up, walked to the entrance of the gun pit, threw the shell away as far as he could and stood and watched. The shell dropped and lay for a few seconds, then burst scattering splinters all over. The officer went to the gunner and told him he was under arrest. Next morning, he was brought in front of the Major and told he didn't know whether to recommend him for a Distinguished Conduct Medal or a District Court Martial. He called him a dammed fool for endangering the lives of his comrades one minute, the next minute he shook his hand and slapped him on the back saying that it was the bravest action he had ever seen. He then reprimanded him severely and told him to be more careful in the future. Gunner Bentley came out of the Major's dugout, lit a fag, started to smile and went to his gun pit to sit down.

Altogether, this particular gun position we were in wasn't what one could call bad or dangerous, probably Mr. Fritz hadn't got our bearings. We did a good deal of firing, particularly at night and just before dawn. One morning during this dawn firing, over came one of Fritz's aeroplanes. As soon as it was seen, the firing was stopped until it went away and every morning after about dawn for a week or so, over would come a German aeroplane, flying very low, in fact, so low that we could see the head of the pilot above the fuselage. Naturally, our Major reported this to headquarters to have a stop put to it, as he didn't want his battery observed or photographed if it could be avoided. Consequently, that same evening our Major made complaints to HQ, an anti-aircraft gun made its position in the rear of our battery on a low lying roadway. The following morning there was to be no firing and everybody who was awake was ready to see the German plane shot down. Sure enough, just as the first streaks of daylight made their appearance in the sky, along came this German aeroplane flying very slow and low. Of course, as soon as it was observed by the aircraft gun, which had been ready and waiting for it, they opened fire with shrapnel shell. The shells burst everywhere, but the place they were intended; such shooting I never saw before, in fact the bullets and splinters from those shells were more dangerous to us and our guns than to the German aeroplane. The German plane just carried out the same stunt he had been using for the past week or so and "coolly" flew away, none the worse.

That particular day I sat down and wrote a letter to my brother, who was in that branch of service (Anti-aircraft), telling him about the shooting being so bad and picking fun out of it. I put the letter into the officer's quarters to be carried along with the others. I was very surprised to receive a visit from one of our officers in connection with this letter, "Did you write this letter Elder", he asked, "Yes Sir", I replied, "it is to my brother", "Oh, is it?" he retorted and continuing he said, "Well look here, if you write any more letters in this strain you'll get into trouble" and with that, he tore the letter into a hundred pieces in front of my eyes.

We didn't stay long in this position after the incident. During one night, we pulled out the guns and moved back to the rear into another position at a place named Knoll Road. This position was just to the right of Sanctuary Wood and in the rear; it was a terrible place to be in. Our guns were placed on ground that was practically levelled by shell holes and the wheels of the guns had to be propped up with beams of wood because our gunners' quarters were so bad, our Major made it an order that only three men had to be at each gun, namely two gunners and an NCO. These men used to make themselves as comfortable as possible in a sort of enlarged shell hole, sandbagged sides and a corrugated iron roof, which wouldn't stop a large stone from coming through, let alone a shell. Our signal dugout was a small German pit with room for only two, who had to be sitting with knees drawn up and head lowered. This Pill Box was situated right in the centre of the six guns and naturally when Mr. Fritz started to shell our guns, we came in for it. The ground in this vicinity was something awful, it was simply shell holes linked together, each one was half full of water, some of which was of a green slimy nature caused by Fritz's gas shells among it. During one sunny day, at dinnertime, there were two signallers, myself and a gunner called McCormack, who was a broad Irishman, whose wit and jolly manner was always a tonic for anybody who was in the "dumps"; he was always rough and ready and would go anywhere, regardless of danger. The four of us had been standing outside our signallers' pit and eating our stew, which was meant for dinner. We had all finished eating and there because no hot water was available to wash up, we had to resort to the nearest water supply to wash our mess tins. Our method of doing this was always to scour out the tin with earth, then wash with water, the nearest water supply was shell holes. The four of us were standing around one hole, which would be about four feet across, we were all stooping down washing our tins in the water, and suddenly there was a loud hiss and explosion. The shell hole water spouted up, drenching us all. I was rubbing my face, realising that a shell had dropped into the very shell hole, which we were standing beside. After I got my face cleaned, I looked at the other three men fully expecting to see some of them killed or wounded, but they were all on their feet. It was a relief to see them, then suddenly, McCormack gave an awful shriek, jumped a few feet into the air and set off across the shell scared ground as fast as he could run. We stood amazed to see him running, because one could hardly walk, never mind run. Here was a man running across this ground which was strewn with barbed wire, pieces of broken trench boards and shell holes half full of water; we couldn't understand it. One of our officers had witnessed this from a distance and came across inquiring if any one was hurt. He was talking to me, pointed to my forehead and said that there was a cut and it was bleeding. It was only a scratch, but he told me to go to the dressing station to have it attended to, in case any poison got into it. I went off to the dressing station, which was only about two hundred yards on the other side of Knoll Road. It was all underground and lit with electric lights. I got into the dressing quarters and was waiting my turn with many others, when I casually looked around and here was McCormack sitting on a bench. I went immediately over to him and said "Hallo Mack, what are you doing here?" he looked but didn't recognise me. His eyes were rolling, hands twitching, he couldn't sit still without fidgeting, looking this way and that, he looked wild. I asked an Orderly what was wrong with him and he told me it was shell shock, so Mack went to hospital, never to be seen again. I got back to my battery and told our officer and pals, everybody was sad about it, because everyone knew that Mack's jolly words, jokes and good humour would be very much missed.

The other two signallers and I who had been in this incident were sent down to the Wagon Line for four days to pull ourselves together. We reached there the same night. The next morning we were shocked to hear that one of our sergeants and two gunners – Sergeant Bogle, Bombardier Tarrant and Gunner Brown[56], had all been killed by a shell at practically the same spot where our affair happened. That afternoon I was told by the Sergeant Major to go to the gun position with a wagon and bring back the dead bodies for burial. We reached the gun position at about 17:00 when dusk was just settling in. The three bodies were wrapped up in their bed blankets and put into the wagon. The two drivers mounted their horses. I got on the seat and started off for the Wagon Line. We hadn't been on our way for two minutes, when Fritz started shelling the road immediately behind us. Knowing full well his methods of creeping along the road with his shells, I told the drivers to trot out their horses a bit faster and eventually, I had to tell them to gallop on account of the shellfire. With the uneven road which was strewn with shell holes partly filled in with stones and the swaying wagon, which had no springs, the three bodies were rolling about the floor, as if they were alive and the blankets in which they were wrapped up became disarranged, exposing their faces and hands. When we eventually got out of the danger area, it was a horrible task the two drivers and I had when we re-wrapped those three men in their blankets; we reached our wagon line and the bodies lay in the wagon all that night. The next morning four men and I went to a small military cemetery, dug three graves and in the afternoon the bodies were brought across and buried just as they were, wrapped up in their blankets, it was a very sad scene to witness. The graves were only about three feet deep on account of the watery nature of the ground; in fact, before the bodies were put in the graves, one could see a thin sheet of water on the surface of the bottom. To make it look a little respectable, the sergeant sprinkled some dry earth over and covered it up.

56 Strangely none of these are listed as being deaths in the Commonwealth War Graves list.

We had been at this Knoll Road position for about three weeks or so and every one of us was absolutely sick of it. The whole place reeked of the dead, particularly horses and mules. Fritz's shelling was most intense. Our dugouts if one could call them so were more like shacks above instead of underground. The roads leading up to this position from the rear were continually under shellfire and our transport suffered accordingly. Water was one of our main difficulties. The usual means employed to bring water up to gun positions was by the water cart, but because the roads were so dangerous, it was impossible to use this method, therefore all water that was brought up for our use was brought up in petrol tins, strapped onto mules and horses backs. These animals were left up along the roads at night time by the drivers. Only a limited supply was brought, just sufficient for cooking purposes, this method was even stopped on several occasions, owing to shelling of the roadway. We suffered a terrible loss of horses through this and matters got into such a state we couldn't rely on any water or ration getting to us. Sometimes, only our bare ration would reach us without water and when this happened, the cooks used to take a walk around the shell holes looking for one that looked clear and clean to fill the Dixie's with. The tea we had for our breakfast with this water was purple in colour and hot to taste, just as if it had been doped with pepper and this was after it had been "sugared and milked". It was just the same if we washed or shaved ourselves, always shell hole water, so we were not sorry when we had to pull out the guns and move our position. As usual, this operation, had to be done in darkness, also owing to the knowledge we had concerning the roads, we were all in a state of nervous apprehension. Eventually, we got on our way, expecting every minute to be caught in Fritz's usual night shelling but for some unaccountable reason, we passed along without anything happening.

We stayed at our Wagon Line for a day, and then off we went again to take our position. We went right through Ypres again onto the Menin Road, a little further along then halted to wait until darkness had settled down properly. We didn't wait long before we were off once again. Right up we went past "Hell Fire Corner" and "Hooge Crater", the only lights being from the stars and moon and the Verey Lights from the trenches. Off the Menin Road onto a sleeper track we went and halted right in the middle of what had once been a large wood. One could see even in the darkness, gaunt stumps of trees standing out like sentinels. Six guns were placed into position alongside this sleeper track, the trail of each gun practically touching the sleepers. This track was a form of road made with railway sleepers laid alongside each other. The usual breadth of these tracks being the length of two sleepers laid end to end, which was usually enough for two wagons to pass each other. This particular track was a supplementary road made across the ground through the wood, called Sanctuary Wood, connecting Menin Road with Knoll Road. The ground near our position was in the usual terrible state with shell holes linked together everywhere. The majority of the shell holes were enormous in size and all half full of water. Our living quarters were captured German Pill Boxes and these were small, just room inside for four men and then they were cramped.

We did a terrible lot of firing both day and night with hard work from the gunners in these bad conditions endured by everybody. Our major issued orders saying every man had to have four days at the gun position and four days at the Wagon Line, it was a relief from the strain on one's nerves being very acceptable to all of us. We had been in this position for about two days when on the second morning at about 10:00 our guns were firing pretty fast. Mr. Fritz was also throwing great dirty "Coal boxes" over. I was beside one of our officers, who was in charge of the firing, when I saw one of Mr Fritz's shells drop right upon our own D Sub Guns trail. When the smoke cleared away and we examined the damage, we couldn't find our sergeant, who had been standing there directing his gunners. He had been literally blown to bits. He was one of the finest men who ever fired a gun, his name was Pat O'Neil[57] who belonged to Dublin, and unfortunately we never found anything of his body. The gun was so badly damaged, it had to be sent away to be replaced.

Life at this position was almost unbearable, during daytime it was foolishness to be in the open, if one wished to be under cover, it was next to impossible owing to the shortage of room available in the Pill Boxes. These Boxes were covered in water, up to three or four inches deep and one's feet were only kept from the water by trench boards, but then it didn't matter so much about wet or dry feet, as we were always plodding about in muddy shell holes. During night, it was nerve racking, total darkness enveloped everything, only the flitting Verey Lights from the trenches casting a sickly glare momentarily over the district. Fritz would send shells over that would crash into the wood, causing awful noises, with the echo's sounding back. Our telephone wires would be broken by splinters, sometimes by the whole shell dropping. Two of us would have to go and mend it. We used to hold the wire between our forefinger and thumb and then let the wire guide us to where it was broken. This generally led us over shell holes and more often into them, sliding down the sides into the slimy water at the bottom. One would lose touch of the wire during these falls then have to find it again, all in pitch darkness. Eventually, we would find the end in a freshly made shell hole, which still reeked of powder and stench from the explosion; the problem was "where was the other end". This made us hunt amongst that terrible ground which had nothing but shell holes of various sizes and depths, all full of water. Plenty of telephone wire lay scattered about, but the question was, who did they belong to and where did they lead? As there were other batteries besides us. The only way possible in darkness to find out the ownership was to connect our telephone we carried with us to all the wires we came across, in the hunt for our own. Sometimes this alone caused us hours of hunting, other times; we would spot

57 Sergeant P. O'Neil was killed on 1 October 1917. He is buried in the Hooge Crater Cemetery. He was 28 years old.

our wire at the first attempt. After repairing and joining the two ends and listening in to find if they were able to speak, we would trudge back to our Battery again, in the darkness, sometimes missing the direction and causing ourselves more trouble, before we eventually reached the guns.

After we arrived back, more often than not, we were greeted with the words "Wires down again", which meant that the other two men had to get out again to mend it. This was a nightly occurrence, Telephonists and Linesmen never had any rest at Ypres district and I was very thankful when I was told to proceed to the Wagon line for my four day relief.

At the Wagon Line, which was situated near Dickebusch[58] we had usual duties to do, such as harness cleaning, grooming horses and generally cleaning equipment. At night we NCO's had to take our turns to go up to the guns with rations and ammunition, which meant four or five hours travelling. We would often leave the Wagon Line about 7.30pm and not get back again until after 1.30am, we then had to be on parade at 6.30am for stable duties. Then again, when one had nothing to do at night, we were always worried about Fritz's bombing aeroplanes, so there wasn't much to choose from between the gun position and the Wagon Line.

My four days were soon over, then, I left the Wagon Line to go to the gun position on foot. I had a reinforcement with me, he was just a young lad who had only been in France for about six weeks, so had never seen a shell burst or fired. I set off about 5pm thinking I would get nicely up to the guns before darkness set in. We got onto the Menin Road and were greeted with Mr. Fritz shelling it. Whole streams of traffic were held up, motor lorries, ammunition wagons and all manner of transport were all standing on the roadside waiting for Fritz to stop. We waited for an hour and still Fritz kept on, I was getting anxious because I knew that if we waited much longer

58 Dickebusch (now Dikkebus) is a village and commune in the province of West Flanders, 5 kilometres South-West of Ypres on the road to Bailleul.

we couldn't reach the guns before darkness. With the prospect of struggling to find the Battery in the darkness, I decided to make a detour across country to avoid the shellfire and at the same time shorten the distance we had to go. We left Menin Road and branched off across country. We got a good way in and could just see Sanctuary Wood in the distance, as the remaining daylight was fading away, I hurried as fast as the ground would allow me, but with no result and eventually we landed on the outskirts of Sanctuary Wood in total darkness. Knowing the Battery was on the sleeper track[59] that cut through the wood, I naturally thought that even in darkness, I would eventually be able to pick up this track by keeping straight on as far as possible, allowing for a zigzag path to avoid the tree stumps. We were well into the wood when to my concern Fritz started shelling. My young companion was understandably very nervous, which wasn't to be wondered at, because of his fear. I decided to reach our guns before darkness. The noise was awful to hear, especially in a wood, where all sounds seemed to be magnified a thousand times. All over we could see reddish yellow glares from the bursting shells, then when two or three came uncomfortably close, I decided to take cover. In the darkness, we couldn't pick and choose, so I changed my mind and resolved to find the track that the Battery was beside. We walked without finding any signs of the sleeper track and eventually because of my companion being in a very nervous state, I took cover in a little broken down corrugated shack. I realised that we were lost and could only wait until daylight. The shelling was becoming more intense and I was rather anxious. We both sat in total darkness in the shack. I shaved splinters off one of the wooden supports of the shack, used some of my letters I had from home and made a fire, which kept going for some considerable time. My companion hugged me close and dozed off to sleep; I awoke feeling fit and as soon as daylight broke, I was up. We both went on feeling cold and haggard. When I

59 A road made from railway sleepers. These were frequently made to go across the shell torn country

was able to take stock of my position, I found we had been going away from the sleeper track all the time. We reached our guns, and then I reported to the Major. He immediately asked me where I had been all the time, as he expected me the previous night. When I told him I had been lost in Sanctuary Wood, he was amazed and said, "It's a wonder that you are here after all that shelling last night".

My next four days gave rise to an outstanding experience. The day before I had to return to the guns from the Wagon Line, the Sergeant Major told me there was a gun to go up. I had to go up with it and take the Gunners' rations with me. At about 5pm I set off with the gun harnessed to six horses. Three drivers and the rations were strapped upon the gun limber, where I sat. We got through Ypres without incident and onto the Menin Road. The road traffic was held up through Mr. Fritz's shelling in the vicinity of Hell Fire Corner, which was a most notorious spot in this district. Dusk was nearing into darkness while we stood and the anxious thoughts of struggling to get the gun up in darkness again worried me greatly. We couldn't do anything other than stand and wait our turn to proceed up the road. There was a great string of motor lorries etc. in front of our gun and if one tried to branch out of this string of traffic, they were immediately pulled up and severely reprimanded by the Traffic Police, therefore we had nothing else to do but wait our turn to move on. Gradually, we moved up to the spot where he was dropping the shells and eventually we were next in turn to make a dash through the area being shelled. Our six horses were fidgeting during the continual shell bursts. I was sitting on the limber waiting until I had a fairly good idea of the interval of time between each successive salvo of shells, which were dropping right in the centre of the road. Right in front of us was a completely clear roadway with great strings of traffic behind us, all anxiously waiting their turn to move on. I was greeted by several unprintable expressions about not moving, but I waited my turn in consideration of my drivers and horses. At last I judged the salvos of Fritz's shells were dropping about every two minutes, so I said to my drivers, "Get ready lads, after the next lot of shells drop, do away as fast as you can make your nags gallop". Over came a salvo and I said, "Now boys, off you go and lash those horses". They didn't need much telling, the short whips were up and down at those horses flanks. We went at breakneck speed with the gun rolling and bumping over the uneven stone road, I had all my work cut out hanging on to the guardrail at the side of the Limber. On we went dashing through the smoke and reek of that salvo of shells that had just dropped. After getting through this, I was horrified to hear the gurgling noise of the succeeding salvo of shells, then I shouted to the driver "Go on, go on, lash 'em". They also heard the noise and were making every effort to get those poor steeds to go faster. Then with a terrible hiss and roar, those four shells passed over us to burst with a terrible explosion on the road we had just passed over a minute or so earlier. We slowed down and eventually stopped to rest our horses after their exertion. These poor beasts were all in a lather from exertion and fear and seemed to understand the danger just as much as us. Because of the impending darkness we didn't stop for more than five minutes or so. We then set off up the road towards Hooge Crater. Knowing this vicinity to be a regular shell dump for Fritz's 5.9s, I halted the horses and considered our best and least dangerous method of getting to the Battery.

On the right side of Menin Road, just before one came to Hooge Crater vicinity, there was a sleeper track that led off the Menin Road at right angles. This track ran right across country on the side of sloping ground and rejoined Menin Road again, a considerable distance beyond Hooge Crater. The one great disadvantage of this track was it had only a one-way route where only one conveyance could get along at a time. Two wagons couldn't pass each other whilst on the track, so if ever a wagon did get stuck after coming off route; it sank into soft ground and were generally left as unsalvageable. Therefore with these points vividly in mind, I stood on the Menin Road and considered whether to proceed up past Hooge Crater or branch off onto the sleeper track and risk meeting any traffic coming from the opposite direction. Mr. Fritz decided the problem for me, when he started "bumping" the Menin Road round about Hooge Crater. Off we went onto the track at walking pace, as this was as much as our horses could do, owing to the uneven level of individual sleepers. Some were lying twisted, others crosswise and a great many broken with shell-fire, so we had to be careful. There was also the gun to consider, as there was only about a couple of feet between the wheels of the gun and the end of the sleepers. We had progressed about half way along the track and were nearing a six-inch Howitzer Battery that was in position alongside the track. We reached this Battery, only to have our spirits squashed. All over the track was the heavy trail of a six-inch Howitzer gun, just allowing room for a man to walk past between the end of the sleepers. The main part of this Howitzer was in the mud with only one wheel on the track; this effectively put a stop to our progress. There wasn't a soul to be seen at this Battery, so obviously we had no assistance to get our gun past. My drivers dismounted, then we all considered what was best. Some of them suggested leaving the gun and driving off with the rations and limber, but I turned it down, knowing that I would be in for it if I did. This gun was needed at the Battery for the following morning. During our talk I had been casting my eyes around and saw a good number of broken sleepers lying about, it was these that gave me my idea. I told one driver to stand by the horses and the other two to come with me. We collected the broken sleepers and widened the track, by laying them next to the sleepers near the Howitzer gun's trail end. We then formed a sort of sidetrack in the form of a half circle jutting out from the main track. It was a flimsy affair, very uneven and took a great deal of time. Darkness was all but set in, just a faint vestige of Verey light remained. When it was finished, I told the drivers to get mounted and emphasised that whatever they did, they must not allow their horses to stop once they had started. I got one of the driver's whips and went to the front two horses took hold of their heads, then guided them in the direction of the track we had just made. I then stood at one side and told the drivers to start to use their whips. I had one whip, which I always used on all the horses. They strained and pulled that gun over those broken sleepers, sometimes the wheels sank with the sleeper they were on. The gun would go over at a dangerous angle and I was losing hope of ever getting it onto the main track, but we succeeded with the tremendous effort of our horses and the poor beasts got nothing for it but flogging with whips. There was no other way, it had to be done. Once we were on the main track, we lost no time and walked as fast as possible, until we reached the end of the sleeper track and so onto the Menin Road again. Once onto the Road, I knew we hadn't far to go. We galloped up the Menin Road in darkness and we hadn't gone far before Fritz started to send some Pip Squeaks over. Luckily, they didn't harm us. We reached the track where the Battery was, then congratulated ourselves with safely reaching our destination. The beginning of this track was downhill, we were proceeding slowly along, with our horses picking their way by instinct more than actual sight, when suddenly, our foremost driver shouted out at the top of his voice "Halt, for Christ's sake, Halt". The remaining two drivers pulled their horses up on their haunches, wondering what was wrong. When I got down to investigate, I was shocked to see why the lead driver had been so concerned about halting. There, even in the darkness, one could see a great gaping hole of tremendous size, right in the centre of the track. By its size I imagine it was possible to put a tramcar into it; how the driver had seen it, I will never know. When I asked him, he said his horses had shied and tried to branch off the track. Our faithful beasts had saved us from a serious accident, which might have meant some of us being severely hurt or even killed. The Battery lay only about fifty yards further along the track, so I told the drivers to wait while I went off to inform my officers of our arrival and the condition of the gun. I was greeted with "Diven't be lang Geordie, we didn't want to stop here". I went off to the Battery and after a struggle and several falls into shell holes, I reached our Major's Pill Box and told him where the gun was. He told me to go to a Second Lieutenant's Pill Box and report to him, I did this with a further struggle with shell hole "baths". Before I left the Major, he told me to report back to him before I left, as he had some orders to take back to the officer in charge of the Wagon Line. The Second Lieutenant and half a dozen gunners were with me to set the gun's position and collect the rations. On reaching the gun, the officer said it was impossible to do anything with it that night, so to get my horses and limber back again. The gun was unlimbered and I told the men to drive so far along the track, then wait for me as I had to get some orders from the Major. I went back again to the Major's Pill Box and collected some papers to take back, then I came back down to the track to meet my drivers. Mr. Fritz was putting some shells over them and I could hear the limber clattering along towards me, up they came at a trot. I shouted at them to stop, but they either didn't see me or took no notice and went straight past. I ran after them as best I could along the track in the darkness and managed to get hold of the back of the gun limber. Suddenly, for some reason unknown to me, the driver left the track and went into Sanctuary Wood. I still hung on to the back shouting for all I was worth for them to stop. I tried to pull myself up onto the seat of the gun limber, but every attempt I made was useless because the gun limber wheels kept dropping into shell holes, causing the whole limber to go adrift making me lose my balance. I eventually let go through sheer exhaustion, and then off it went vanishing into the darkness, so I was left on my own. It was obvious that the drivers were at fault; they should have waited for me because I was the NCO in charge and had ordered them to meet me. My intentions had been to meet them on the track, as I had informed them, and then proceed until we came onto the Knoll Road, thus avoiding the Menin Road again. The drivers had taken it unto themselves to go their way, which was along an earth track that ran through the edge of Sanctuary Wood. If I had been with them, I would never have allowed them to go that way. The place was littered with shell holes broken wagons and dead horses etc., all providing ample evidence of shellfire. I stood on that earth track in complete darkness with Mr. Fritz shelling all around, I immediately said to myself, no Wagon Line for me tonight, and then I made my way back to the Battery again. I went to a large Pill Box that was occupied by our D Sub Section to tell them what had happened. I then asked if I could stop there for the night. I should have reported the matter to my Officer, but what with the state of the ground, the darkness, Fritz's shelling and not to mention my state of mind after being left behind by the drivers, I completely forgot, I got into the Pill Box sat on an upturned petrol tin in the doorway, just behind the gas blanket. Because the roof was so low, when I bent down, my chin touched my chest, my feet were up to my uppers in water and my knees were drawn up tight to my body. I sat in this uncomfortable position, dozing until daylight broke. When I got outside, I could hardly stand up, my feet were so cramped, but eventually I made my way to the Wagon Line. I went back by way of Hooge Crater and Menin Road and arrived at the Wagon Line at about 9 am. The Sergeant Major was in the Horse Line when I approached and he immediately stopped me, "Well, where's the Gun Limber" he asked in a surly manner. His question surprised me very much, as I naturally thought they would have been back last night. He again asked "Where's the Limber and where have you left it?" I told him what had happened and he said I should have stayed with them. I then started to go to my little shack, but he stopped me and blurted out "Well, there are the pack mules ready to go up with the ammunition. I want you to go up with them now". I nearly dropped where I stood, I said that I had already been out all night and had a hard task in getting the Gun up and about and hadn't had anything to eat since 3.30pm the previous day. I also asked to see the Major first, who came down to the Wagon Line on horseback. I asked the Sergeant Major to take me to the Major. He refused to do this, so I informed him I would go myself then made my way to the house the Major was staying in whilst he was at the Wagon Line. I saw his Servant and asked him to see if the Major would speak to me. After a few minutes, I was standing beside the Major who was sitting in an armchair. He asked me what I wanted. I told him everything that had happened since I had left the Wagon Line the previous day. I finished with the account of the Sergeant Major wanting me to go straight back to the Gun position with pack mules and ammunition. I also added that I wasn't refusing to go back, only that I would like some rations before I left. The Major sat and listened to me patiently, without interrupting. When I had finished my story, he shouted to his Servant to bring the Sergeant Major. The Sergeant Major walked in, saluted and stood to attention, "Oh, Sergeant Major" the Officer began "Bombardier Elder informs me that you want him to go back to the Gun positions immediately, is that so?" "Yes, Sir", he said, "Haven't you another NCO available?" the Major asked "Yes, Sir, but I want Elder to go on account of the Limber which is missing". Then the Sergeant Major went on to say that I had gone the previous afternoon to take a Gun to the Gun position and didn't come back until 9am that day. In the meantime the three men I was with had returned at 4am with only 5 horses. They told him that Bombardier Elder had told them he would meet them on the Sleeper Track, they said they hadn't seen him and because of Fritz's shelling, they didn't want to stand on the track in case they got hit and so thought it best for them to come back straight away. This they did and reached Sanctuary Wood. When they came out of the Wood, Fritz was shelling heavily and one shell had dropped right on the Gun Limber smashing it and blowing off one wheel, killing one of the horses. They had changed tracks to come back with the five other horses. The Sergeant Major then added that he wanted me to go back again, mainly to find where the Gun Limber was, to bring it back. The Major sat in silence for a while, then turned and faced me. "Bombardier Elder" he said, "I congratulate you on your work in getting that Gun up to the position under the difficulties you have had", he then said to the Sergeant Major, "See that Bombardier Elder has a good meal, then excuse him from duties for 24 hours and find another NCO to take up the pack mules". The Sergeant Major and I went to the Quarter Master's Stores where I was given a tin of "Mackconicks", half a loaf of bread, butter and cheese and he told the cook to make me some tea. He did this and with my stock of provisions, I had a good tuck in and felt well satisfied with myself. The Gun Limber was brought back later by another NCO and the same three drivers. When I saw it, I patted myself on the back at having had such a lucky escape from certain death.

We stayed at the Sanctuary Wood position for some considerable time assisting in every attack that was made on the Passchendaele Ridge positions, which were held by the Germans. We were continually firing barrages and SOS's, so after four days duty at the guns it was impossible to get any sleep. If we did manage to snatch a nap, we still seemed to hear shell bursts and gun firing; it was so impressed upon our nerves. Everyone seemed to move in a continual state of apprehension, always expecting shells and noises of shells bursting, it was enough to turn one's brain at times. Even the drivers who used to come up every night were somewhat in the same condition. They used to bring up ammunition on mules and horse back with a canvas overlap flung across and strapped to the saddles. On each canvas there were eight pockets and into each pocket was inserted the nose of an 18 pounder shell, thus making each animal carry sixteen shells, which were some considerable weight. One driver had two animals to lead up to the guns and the job of loading two mules with ammunition strapped to their back wasn't easy. When they did eventually reach the Guns with the shells, they didn't waste time getting them off. After doing this, they gave one of their animals a kick or whip across its flanks and chased it away. The driver got upon the other one's back and followed it; off they went at a gallop, even in darkness. Every time each horse or mule they had chased away was back at the Wagon Line, standing patiently in its place at the horse line, before the actual driver; thus showing the instinct of these faithful beasts, in getting back to where they belonged, without human aid.

One night, we were ordered to leave the position, we all had visions of going back into the areas among the green fields and civilian houses, as there had been consistent rumours of such things. Eventually, we pulled out the guns and left the position at dusk, Mr. Fritz's observation balloons were high in the sky and we expected a good thrashing, but fortunately it never came off. We came into the Menin Road and all along the single track from where I had previously brought the gun and rations. We were slowly walking along this track when my Officer said to me "There's a moke standing over there", pointing to a spot about fifty yards away over the shell holed ground. "We might as well rope him in, as he is on his own". Off I went with a Gunner and we reached it in a few minutes, when I looked at him I was filled with pity for that poor mule who stood on three legs, with the right foreleg off the ground. On examination I saw a large hole in its right shoulder, which was also very swollen and it was trying to nibble at a little clot of grass which was sticking out of the soggy ground. This was without exaggeration, the only bit of grass that I could see in the vicinity, the whole affair was so sorrowful. Seeing us standing by the mule without handling it, my Officer came across and said "Poor devil", then he drew a revolver, stood about six feet away, aimed at the mule's head and fired. The mule dropped stone dead where it stood, after eating its last meal of half a dozen blades of grass; such was war to our dumb friends.

We reached our Wagon Line late that night and were all glad to have a chance of a decent lie down. We had about a week of general cleaning up, guns, harnesses, and horses etc., were thoroughly overhauled and off we went again, bag and baggage. We marched all day and eventually put up on the outskirts of Poperinge. We had a few free nights at this large place as well as some relaxation, we had beer, Vin Blanc, Vin Rouge, Benedictine and made merry while it lasted, which wasn't long. We moved off again and finally pitched our Wagon

Line at Elverdinge Rail Head, we weren't here long, before the guns were once more on their way up to the firing line, then were settled in a position directly in front of Houthulst Forest[60], which was in German possession. Although we were about a mile and a half away from this crest, we could see it sticking on the skyline like a foreboding black barrier, which in reality was the correct description of it, as it had resisted many capture attempts by our troops.

As in our previous position, our guns were on a sleeper track, the state of the ground not allowing for a proper gun emplacement to be made. The nature of the place was such that no man was allowed to be at those guns, except for firing purposes. The wisdom of these regulations was often vividly illustrated to all of us. The periods of Fritz's shellfire were very erratic and every time he started to shell, it was for about 15 minutes duration. His shellfire was always concentrated upon the sleeper track the guns were on; they were always getting damaged by splinters and had to be eventually replaced. Our Gunners were billeted in captured German Pill Boxes, which were very large and roomy, but they had great difficulty in reaching the guns in darkness. Whenever there was an SOS, which necessitated every gun on that particular front opening fire, the Gunners had to leave their Pill Box and scramble across awful shell holed ground. This always resulted in the Batteries opening fire spasmodically and in turn would minimise the aid to the Infantry.

One fine day, I was returning from an observation post with my Officer, where we had been to register some SOS lines. We had just reached the track that the Battery was on, when we heard an awful racket of machine gunfire. We looked up and saw one of our aeroplanes, it was one of those large slow craft used for artillery observation. Two red German planes were swooping over, around and underneath the British plane, firing their machine guns for all

60 The forest just to the North East of Ypres and beyond Passchendaele was occupied by the Germans on 21st October 1914 and remained in their hands until the Ypres offensive of 1917. This is now the site of a large Belgium military cemetery.

they were worth. Our plane wasn't slow in answering them back, but the odds were too great, so our Pilot was forced to come down. He came down as gently as possible, but the nose of the plane struck the ground and the tail canted up about fifty yards away from where we stood. The two German planes still flew around firing their machine guns at our grounded plane. Our two men who were still in their plane kept firing back as best they could. We were very interested spectators to this uneven battle. I was cursing those two Germans for bad sportsmanship. They weren't satisfied in getting our plane down to the ground, but had to persist in trying to kill the men that were in it, but the underdog got the better of them, even though this plane was grounded. The Germans were still flying around giving some terrible machine gun bursts at our plane, but we gave a continuous burst on the machine gun with great effort. One of the German planes burst into flames then dropped about two hundred yards away and was raging with fire a few moments later. Seeing this happen, the other gunman turned tail and went off flying low to escape the anti-aircraft. My Officer and I then went across to our plane, when we approached, the two occupants were getting out, both dressed in overalls and the usual flying dress. One of them who I thought was an officer, said to my Officer, "Near call that Major, but we got one of them, let's go across to their plane". The four of us then proceeded over to where the German plane was blazing, we couldn't get close owing to the severe heat. We came to the conclusion that the Pilots must have been killed long ago. The two airmen went with us to our Officer's Pill Box and had a wash and something to eat before they proceeded back to the aerodrome.

The Pill Box we Signallers had was massive, there were two large rooms about eight-foot square and two others at about five foot square. Four officers occupied two and we Signallers occupied the other two, using them for sleeping quarters and telephone control; we also had the Officer's servants in with us. A rather amusing incident occurred with one of the Major's servants, he had been having an awful struggle one wet evening to make a meal for the Major, the only wood he had was damp and naturally very hard to burn. He made some coffee and fried steak, which the Major ate and was waiting for his savoury, which consisted of a few sardines spread on toast. The fire was out and the remaining wood was hopelessly damp for relighting, so he was at his wits end as to how he could get the toast made. He was walking about the Pill Box scratching his head and coming out with some unprintable remarks about Officers. All us Signallers and Officers' Servants were laughing and kidding him about it, Meanwhile, the Major's servant put a slice of bread on the mushy white embers of the burnt wood and stooped down with his mouth close to the fireplace and started to blow. With the continued blowing, small red embers started to appear among the white ones. After keeping this up for about five minutes, the slice of bread was taken off, there were small spots here and there over the surface. After dusting it with a cloth, the Servant spread the sardines over it and cut it into small pieces, put it onto a clean enamel plate then took it to the Major. Back he came again all smiles and said to us "Where there's a will, there's a way" and the Major knew no more. Shortly after this incident, I received orders from my Major to choose another Signaller to proceed with me back to the rear on a certain day and report to the Corps Signalling School to learn how to use a new signalling telephone. After considering all the Signallers in my charge, I chose a young chap who was in his teens to go with me. He hadn't been with us very long, so he wasn't used to the firing line, therefore I thought I would give him a bit of relief by taking him with me. Eventually, the appointed day arrived and the two of us left the guns to proceed to the rear. We walked all the way back along duck board tracks that zigzagged over the shell-seared ground. There was only room for one person to walk along at a time; I was in front with my mate close to my heels. We trudged along like this for a considerable distance until we were nearing the positions of our big Howitzer. I noticed that Fritz was putting some awful big shells over, which were falling in front of us, but quite a long way off. Knowing the duck board track we were walking along took a big sweep to the right, I naturally judged that we would be well out of the line of fire as we proceeded; I made it my business to keep an eye on those shells all the same. As we passed along the track, we went well away to the right and eventually got in line with the shells, which Fritz was putting over. The shells were bursting well away on our left, so we were very calm about it. Suddenly, to my horror, I heard the close sounding gurgling of 5.9 shells coming towards us, with my long experience, I knew instantly that they would burst somewhere near us. I shouted at the top of my voice "Get down kid quick" and at that, I then dived down on my stomach flat on the duckboards and covered my head with my tin hat. There was then an awful roar, crash and a tremendous explosion, with shells dropping on our left, about four or five yards from the duckboards. The lumps of earth were still falling when I jumped up on my feet again, calling to my mate to run for a German Pill Box that lay about fifty yards in front of us. I ran towards the Pill Box. I hadn't got six yards, before I was greeted with a haunting sort of nervous cry "Geordie, Geordie, I'm hit", my mate faltered. I immediately turned around and saw him staggering to his feet, he rose up on one knee and fell again, I simply got hold of him, half carried and half dragged him along towards that Pill Box. Fritz was still putting them over and was uncomfortably close, but I didn't pay much attention, because I was preoccupied with my mate. I struggled on and eventually reached the Pill Box, got inside and was relieved to find two men who were RGA[61] Signallers, who helped me to lay him on one of their beds. We put him on his stomach, and bared his back. In the vicinity of his kidneys, were two holes about half an inch long, one hole at each side of his spine and sticking out of the right side was a small shell splinter. I got my field dressing out, covered my forefinger and thumb with the bandage, took hold of the splinter, gave it a quick pull and out it came. I then covered both wounds with Iodine from the little glass phials that were in our field

61 Royal Garrison Artillery.

dressings. My mate winced terribly during this, as it smarted him greatly, eventually I had him trussed up as comfortable as possible. The poor fellow was suffering awful pain but he kept up wonderful, never a tear did he shed, even though he was practically a boy. The colour of his face was making me anxious. He was awful to look at, to me his face was greenish white. I asked the two RGA men how far the nearest Aid Post was and they told me about three kilometres. I then asked if one of them would give me a hand to get my mate there, but neither of them could leave their post, so I went outside to see if I could get anyone to give assistance. Several Infantrymen came hurrying past, but everyone I asked hadn't time or was on important business. I hunted around the vicinity and found a blood stained stretcher lying in a shell hole so I took it to the Pill Box, put my mate on it and made him comfortable. I had just finished when I saw an officer and a dozen or so Infantrymen coming along another duck board track. It wasn't long before I was standing to salute beside the Officer "Sir" I said, "I have a wounded pal in the Pill Box back there and can't get any assistance to get him to Hospital as he's pretty badly hit". "How many men do you want Bombardier?" he asked. "One will do Sir" I answered and at that, he ordered one man to fall out and come with me. Together, this Infantryman and I carried my mate on the stretcher about three kilometres to the Aid Post, I saw him attended to and I posted a field postcard at the Aid Post to his mother telling her that her son was wounded and in Hospital but was doing well. I then saw my mate put on a light railway, which was used for the wounded and said goodbye. He eventually reached a London Hospital and wrote to tell me that the postcard I had written was the first news his mother had received about him being hit. It was a month after she had received my postcard, when she received official notice of her son from the War Office

Having seen my mate off to Hospital, I made my way to receive instructions regarding the new telephone. Because of the time it took to look after my mate, I found that the class of Signallers who had attended the place of instruction had all finished and gone, except for the Instructor. After explaining the reason for my late arrival, the Instructor gave me a rough outline of the new telephone and notes of its construction, saying it was the best he could do. I left him and went to our Wagon Line to stay the night and report about my mate being in Hospital; the following morning I went back to the Battery.

The weeks that followed were all the same, continual firing of guns on both sides, attacks and counter attacks. We had awful jobs to do, mainly at night, so sleep was out of the question. Our wet clothes were always a source of complaint and anxiety. The conditions were very bad for the horses, never mind the men, who one after another were falling sick and going to Hospital and I was also soon to become a victim of the conditions. For days and nights I had an awful pain in my legs and back, but carried on as best I could because I didn't want to go to Hospital. I knew it would mean leaving the Battery for good and eventually going to another one. Night after night I had no sleep, sometimes I was out on broken wires in darkness and mud, other times in bed, not able to sleep for pain. One night at about 8pm I was on duty at the telephone in the Pill Box, when the Officer sent his servant in to tell me to go in for the rum ration. I got up from the telephone to get an enamel pot which would hold a pint and a half, I had to get eight Signallers and four servants' rations in it. I went to the Officer who said I wasn't looking well and advised me to get some rest, I half smiled, but said nothing, as an idea came into my head. I went back with little over a pint of rum, laid it on a table and sat down at the telephone with my head on my arms, my legs and back were all aches and pains. One of the servants got the rum, filled it up with hot water, put in plenty of sugar, stirred it, took a sip and handed it around to the others; only two took a sip but others who were very young didn't want any. The pot reached me with about a pint of neat rum inside, I took hold of it and lifted it to my mouth, all of them were watching me, I think they must have sensed what was on my mind. I looked at the contents and said, "I'll bloody well sleep tonight", put my lips to the pot and drank until I was out of breath, there wasn't much left when I put it down. I sat a little longer feeling all of a glow when the telephone started to buzz, I picked it up, but something seemed to go wrong, I bashed it down onto the table and said "To hell with it", then something seemed to snap in my head and all was black – I knew no more. They put me to bed and I slept right through the night and well into the next afternoon, they had tried to rouse me, but couldn't. When I did wake up, I felt a thousand times worse with pains from head to foot. The Major sent for me to go with him up to the Observation Post in the trenches, I was unsteady but went to the Major's Pill Box. As soon as he saw me, he told me to go to the Wagon Line straight away and see the Doctor. I was so weak, I had to give in. I waited for the rations to come in one of our wagons as soon as darkness set in, then went back to the Wagon Line. Unable to see the Doctor that night, I had to wait until 9am the next day and was in a sorry state when I arrived at the Doctor's tent. He looked at me and said "Report to the field ambulance tents in half an hour". After being examined by a Doctor, I was put into a Red Cross motor and went along the roads to the back areas. We eventually stopped at a large Red Cross Hospital, on the outskirts of Proven[62], with mainly huts and several large tents. It wasn't long before I was cleansed and snugly tucked into bed in a nice long roomy hut. The next day my temperature was very high, my pains seemed to be worse and the medicine was the usual pills, pills, pills. My food was very thick "Glaxo", a dried milk food, which was given for breakfast and dinner. My health varied very little during the next fortnight, but in the third week, I seemed to quickly pick up.

After a day or two walking about the hut I was told to stay up all day and get outside into the fresh air. It was during my walks outside around the Hospital grounds when I noticed my hut was the last in a row of ten and next to it there was a large tent with approximately forty patients. On the Thursday night of the third week we could

62 14 kilometres NW of Poperinge

hear overhead the drone and tug-tug of Fritz's bombers coming towards us, at first we thought it was imagination, but not so this time. Without the slightest warning, there were terrible explosions close to our hut, which made our beds jump off the floor, then we all got up, even those poor chaps who were severely wounded. Because all the lights were out, we struggled to find our way past the beds to the door, but fortunately, we were stopped by nurses and RAMC Orderlies and told to get back into bed immediately. All we knew of the effects of the explosions, which were so close, was continual moaning and screeching. On the next day we were allowed to go outside and what a sight met our eyes, the large tent was lying tattered and torn just as if some gigantic knife had ripped it to shreds, but worse still, we could see remains of what had been neat Hospital beds with patients in them. Evidence of carnage was all over, legs and arms or sometimes a body sticking out of the mangled mass of bedsteads and canvas, it was sickening to witness. I was told that nearly every patient in that tent was killed, including several nurses.

I was very much relieved to find out that I was to be discharged on the Saturday to go back to my Battery. I left Proven about 10 o'clock on Saturday morning, having been told by the RTO[63] that my Unit was still in Elverdinge, where our Wagon Line was. I stepped out feeling rather pleased with myself for feeling so fit, I eventually reached Poperinge about dinnertime. As I had a little money, I thought I would stay the weekend and enjoy myself, before I went back to that Godforsaken firing line. I went to the pictures and concerts at the YMCA etc., until night and then slept in the YMCA until morning, then I set off to my Wagon Line at Elverdinge, 10 or 12 kilometres away. I managed to jump motor Lorries a good part of the way and eventually arrived near our Wagon Line at about 3.30pm. I made my way to my pal's well-known shack, pushed the door open, tossed my kit down and sat on it. I looked around and was astounded to find that I didn't know any of them. Naturally, I was full of questions

63 Railway Transport Officer

and found out they were the 112 Bde. RFA and not my mob. They hadn't any knowledge of my Brigade so couldn't help me. I explained that this was where I had left my pals when I went to Hospital about three weeks' ago. They said they had been there a fortnight relieving a Howitzer Brigade, so it seemed that my Brigade had left a day or so after me. After a good deal of thought, I decided it would be better for me to go back to Poperinge than to look for my Battery. No doubt, I could have gone back to where my Battery had been, but the possibility of not finding them there was apparent. Therefore I decided it was best for me to retrace my steps to Poperinge without further delay and was lucky to jump motor Lorries the best part of the way.

Darkness was just setting in, when I arrived beside the station. I stood for a while wondering what to do, because I had nowhere to rest for the night. Eventually, I went to the RTO's office in the station after asking for my Battery's whereabouts, I was told to go to the rest camp outside the station and report back at 8am the next morning. I proceeded to the rest camp finding it to be no more than a few Nissan huts in a bad state of repair. I went to one hut with the only place available for me to lie down near the doorway. Because there was no door, it was a very draughty place to lie down. I only had my overcoat for warmth and tossed and turned for a long time. There was no light, only sometimes someone would light a candle.

Well into morning, Fritz's bombers came and dropped tons of bombs around the station, each bomb, caused the corrugated iron of the hut to rattle and crack, just as if it were going to fall to pieces. They often dropped so near and I fully expected one to drop on the hut and clear matters up. Sleep was out of the question and long before 8am I was standing around to put the time in, I was cold, hungry and miserable. Continually passing through my thoughts was the contrast of my present circumstances to that of a week or so previous, when I was snug in a Hospital bed. As 8am drew near, I made my way to the station, where there was a long line of soldiers standing waiting their turn to see the RTO's, regarding their unit's whereabouts. Nearly all these men had just returned from leave and like me, were stranded. My turn came at last to go to the RTO's office where there was a Corporal being seen just before me. The Officer asked him what unit he wanted and he replied "29th Division Sir", the Officer pulled a long face with a sarcastic smile and told the Corporal to go to Germany. I learned that the majority of the 29th Division had either been captured or wiped out at Cambrai a few weeks ago, so this was just another act of fate with this Corporal being on leave in England when the 29th Division was smashed up. Having disposed of the Corporal, the Officer turned to me and I told him I wanted the 315th Bde. RFA. He asked me where I had been and I said Elverdinge, "Who sent you down there?" he asked. I said "the RTO at Proven Station had done so", "Dammed Fool" was all I could hear from the Officer. He then told me my Unit was beside Arras, hundreds of miles away and to report back again in about two hours to get the train to Boulogne. He dismissed me and called for the next man, I interrupted him with "What about some rations Sir?", I told him I had had nothing since I left Hospital the previous morning, so he gave me an order to go to the store to draw 24 hours rations. It didn't take me long to get bacon, tea, sugar, cheese, butter, a loaf of bread and a tinned dinner. I managed to make breakfast and got the hot water to make my tea from an engine standing in the station. Eventually, I left Poperinge in the usual mode of troop travel, cattle trucks and after an uneventful journey of some twenty hours, I reached Boulogne. I was sent to the rest camp at St. Martins and remained there for three days before I was pushed off again on the train to Arras.

Recovering an 18 pounder gun from the Flanders mud

18 pounder in action

Waiting for orders

Batteries on the move

Battery coming away from a bombardment

18 pounder gun

Recruitment poster, which might have inspired George

Pencil drawing by Gilbert Holliday of a Signaller at work

I eventually arrived and after some considerable hunting and wandering around, I found my Battery Wagon Line about four kilometres outside Arras. I had been away for nearly a month. I was sent to the gun position the next morning and it was a very dreary desolate place, right in the wilds. There wasn't any sign of a house, or even ruins, no trees or grass, just one mass of brown shell seared earth, with the white chalk tops of the opposing trenches standing out in the foreground. We did very little firing and after a fortnight, we pulled out the guns and came to the Wagon Line. For the next week or so we did nothing, only clean up. Christmas 1917 came and went, just like any other day, but on New Year's Eve 1918, at about half past six, a group of twenty of us arranged to go to the village of Agincourt[64] about a mile away. It was a lovely night, the moon was full and casting a light over the snow covered countryside. As we were passing through the Wagon Line, the Sergeant Major came out of his tent and shouted at the top of his voice "Rum up", Oh, what a dash, "Come on lads" the Sergeant Major said, "An extra tot tonight, New Year's Eve, you know". We all had a liberal supply and set off across the fields towards the village in good spirits, both inside and out. We cut across country for quickness and also to avoid the icy roads as much as possible, which made it very difficult to walk. We reached Agincourt at about 7.30pm and from then until 10pm we had plenty of splendid jollification, white wine was flowing like water, champagne bottles were popping all over and singing and dancing was the order of the day. The last thing I truly remembered was struggling to get out of the Estaminet (pub) door, with a cane chair over each arm. The following morning I woke up to find myself lying on the ground, still fully dressed with spurs etc., inside a big hut, which was used to

64 George was evidently completely ignorant of the significance of Agincourt. The Battle of Agincourt, spelled Azincourt by the French, one of England's most famous battles took place on the 25th of October 1415 in Northern France near the villages of Agincourt and Tramecourt. This battle between the English led by King Henry V and the French lead by the Constable d'Albret was a total victory for the English who were outnumbered by almost 6 to 1.

accommodate about a hundred men. The two chairs were lying partly broken and at one end of the hut were broken beds or wooden bunks. I got up and pulled myself together and asked a driver how I came to be lying there. He told me that the whole party of us who went to Agincourt had returned about midnight in an intoxicated state, some being worse than others. I had been one of the worst and had eventually carried the two cane chairs along the icy roads, falling down and getting up, but still retaining the chairs. We reached the hut at about midnight when I threw the chairs down on the floor. The majority in the hut were in bed and the disturbance had roused everyone inside, some of them had started to kid me about the chairs I had brought, saying I had tried to climb up the bunks on the top row of beds. With my weight added to those who were hanging over the sides of the top beds, the whole row of about 24 beds came toppling over onto the floor. Naturally, there had been some nasty knocks, but everything had been taken in good spirits. I then went out of the hut into the dark stables, hunted amongst the horses and mules, got hold of the Battery Pet, who was a little mule called Baby and rode into the hut shouting that here was their "First Foot". After this account, I wondered how I had escaped being kicked to death by the horses, as it must have been inky black inside the stables. This passed over without anyone being punished, probably because it was New Year.

Matters went along somewhat quiet until one Sunday early in January. We had finished our usual duties of harness cleaning and attending to the horses and wagons etc., and were standing in our ranks, prior to being dismissed for dinner. The Sergeant Major and Officer were standing in front of the ranks and the Sergeant Major shouted "Battery, Attention", then said "The Battery will parade again at 2pm for harness cleaning, "Dismiss" and we broke away with discontent pictured on our faces. It had been the custom that when we were not in action or actually fighting, we always had Sunday afternoon to ourselves and with the Sergeant Major's announcement coming as it did, we very much resented it. Dinner passed over and

2pm drew nigh, bugles sounded the "fall in", but curiously enough no one made a move from their little shacks or tent to fall in on parade. The Sergeants and NCOs went around the shacks etc., ordering the men to fall in on parade and eventually after a half hour or so, the parade was formed, then the Major put in an appearance. After severely lecturing us about punishments etc., for disobeying orders, he ordered us to march to the stables to do harness cleaning. Sergeants in charge of each subsection then took charge of their men, gave the order right turn; no one moved, again the orders were given, but still not a man moved. One would naturally think we had previously arranged all this, but as true as I live today to write this, no word was breathed by any man regarding our actions on this day. It just seemed as if every man resented this Sunday afternoon work and was fed up. After a consultation between our Major and other Officers, we were informed that every man would be confined to camp during the rest of our stay at the Wagon Line and so ended that Sunday's harness cleaning. This punishment didn't affect us to any extent, as it only lasted a week.

Chapter 8

The German March Offensive

At 4.40 on the morning of 21st March 1918 the German Artillery shook the front between Vimy and Soissons firing some 3 million rounds. This was the beginning of the German March Offensive, Operation Michael, which made enormous gains not seen on the Western Front war before. On the first day the Germans had inflicted 38,000 casualties on the British and taken 21,000 prisoners. The British 5th Army retreated in much disorder for the next week. Albert among other towns were taken and more sickening all the gains from the Battle of the Somme were lost in a trice. But by 25th April the Germans had reached their culminating point and were in short overstretched and the slow recapture of lost ground began.

One day in about the third week in January 1918 we were ordered to pack up and be ready to march off at 6am the following day. We marched at a fast pace, the whole Brigade together, no one being allowed to ride on the gun or wagons. The only persons riding were the Officers, Sergeant Major, Sergeants, Corporals and drivers of gun and wagon teams; the ordinary Gunners and Signallers had to use "Shank's Pony". The weather was awful on the first two days, snow, sleet and wind, each night we pulled into some field and had to make the best of it, sometimes laying down in wet clothes. Our meals consisted of Bully Beef and biscuits, changed with jam and cheese. We marched for four days, passing through the devastated countryside and eventually through Perrone and Bapaume. Our wagons and baggage were left behind to form a base then the guns and Gunners etc., went on and eventually got into position, in front of St. Quentin. Four of our guns were placed in Holnon Wood[65] with the other two placed in a position at crossroads about half a mile away, the whole lot bearing on St. Quentin and district.

From the beginning of February until the beginning of March, the weather improved, wonderful lovely sunshine and summer-like conditions. The only shells we fired were used for registering the six guns, no night firing was done with no trench duty for us Signallers, in fact we were enjoying ourselves immensely. Our rations were awful, but we had ample opportunity to supplement these by buying eggs, beer, biscuits, custard etc., from various canteens, which were dotted about the district. There was one particular day that we couldn't get anything from the canteen and were so hungry that I and another two men went around the other Batteries (of which there were very few) begging ordinary biscuits, not meeting with much success, as they were always hungry.

The day came when we were ordered out of action to go for a rest into the back areas, we were very sorry to leave such a cushy place and reluctantly pulled our guns out to allow another Battery to take our place. This position was the extreme right flank of the British Army in France, our neighbours being French 75's[66]. We left this lovely district of summer conditions, green grass, trees, flowers etc., and

---

65 Holnon is a village 6 kilometres west of St Quentin and south of the main road to Vermand and Amiens. Holnon village and wood were the scene of heavy fighting between the 6th Division and the enemy on the 14th-19th September, 1918. This was yet to occur.

66 French 75 was the 75mm artillery piece which had a fearsome reputation and was probably the finest field artillery gun of the era. After the war a cocktail was made to mark its reputation and can still be found in cocktail books as "French 75".

moved back along the roads where we had previously been. The whole Brigade was on the move again and while we were travelling, a motorcycle dispatch rider overtook us and went to our Colonel at the head of the Brigade. We were halted and after a half an hour were ordered to immediately turn about, this was done with considerable trouble, as no wagon or gun could turn as it stood. Each separate vehicle had to be unlimbered, then hitched up again. After every gun and wagon had been turned, we set off back again towards St. Quentin, every one of us was wondering what the reason was for this sudden change of plan. Rumours came from somewhere, God only knows where, that Fritz had broken through and various stories and accounts were on the men's' lips. Late that day however, each Battery left the main road and went to their respective place allotted to them by the Colonel. We eventually finished our travelling at some crossroads close to the ruined village of Vaulx, which was about six kilometres from St. Quentin. Our guns were put into position in a green field, which was considerably below the level of the road, which ran up hill on the right, the crossroads and village were about a hundred yards behind us. Our "B" Battery took up a position about four hundred yards directly in front of us. Our guns were covered with camouflage of wire netting and coloured pieces of cloth to represent the surrounding ground. Gunners made themselves as comfortable as possible and we twelve Signallers had a large wagon waterproof sheet, which was used to make our Quarters. We had barely got fixed up when I was instructed to get hold of all the telephone wire I had and bring at least six Signallers with me, then report to our Signalling Officer as soon as possible. We started to lay this wire at our Battery going right past our "B" Battery, across country in the direction of St. Quentin. We passed through lovely countryside, everything summer-like and no sign of war. There was complete absence of shell bursts or rifle fire, in fact it was impossible to imagine there was a war in progress. Dusk was rapidly setting in when we reached the outskirts of a large wood. We had to make large detours to lay the wire owing to great belts of barbed wire, which stretched right across country as far as the eye could see. These belts were about ten yards in breadth, with open spaces in the wire to allow passage through and it was to these open spaces that we had to take the wire to make any progress. These detours were pretty numerous and consequently our wire didn't last as long as it would otherwise have done by travelling in a straight line, so eventually, we found ourselves with no more wire, and then darkness set in. After fixing up our telephone to the wire we had just reeled out, our Officer got in touch with the Major at the Battery. After explaining the position, the Major said he would immediately have six Gunners bring more wire to us, then he would instruct them to follow the track of our wire from the Battery. He also said our Officer had to send six men along the wire to meet the Gunners, to get the wire so that they could return to the Battery without delay. It was a lovely moonlit night, but rather cold, not a sound could be heard except queer noises from the wood. The Verey lights could be seen in the far distance, but no gun firing could be heard. It was a strange atmosphere that seemed to prevail; just as if one expected something dreadful to happen suddenly, in fact it gave us a creepy feeling. We smoked, walked about, sat down and were generally uneasy, but didn't really know the reason. My Officer told me that the work we were doing had to be finished before dawn, as our people expected Mr. Fritz to make a big attack about then, which was the reason why the Brigade had been turned back. Our six signallers arrived with two large reels of wire, then after they had some rest, we started to lay the wire out. Our Officer took his turn at holding the reel; we skirted the wood for a good distance, then cut through a fringe into a railway cutting and went right along until it ended at a part where the railway ran into open country. Our wire was taken up the sides of the railway embankment into a little corrugated iron hut and fixed up with a telephone; in all we had laid six miles of wire that night. We all sat down in the hut while our Officer got through to the Battery, he spoke quite clearly to the Major which proved that the wire had been well and truly laid. Our Major gave us orders to stay there until recalled, some of the Signallers had to look to the wire immediately if communication failed, but on no account had it to be disconnected. The wire had to be kept in good order at all costs, naturally these orders made us think, surely something big must be coming off, leaving us all pins and needles. The Infantry Officers kept popping into our hut and talking in low tones to an Officer. They all had a grave expression on their faces. Occasionally, we heard men tramping past along the gravel of ballast on the railway lines. An Officer kept looking over towards where Fritz's lines were, as if he expected something, but only Verey lights were to bc seen. As dawn approached, there was a hushed expectance in the air; still not any unusual sounds could be heard. Daylight arrived, sun shone brightly and birds sang, but still no gun firing, just a fine summer's morning in lovely countryside. Our telephone buzzed and the Major spoke, "Come in at once" was our order, so we left and trudged back to the Battery, Fritz's expected attack hadn't come.

For a few days, we did absolutely nothing but clean ourselves and equipment and the Gunners looked after their guns. One day our Major told me to get my Signallers to make an emplacement into the bank side, it had to be small, strong and well concealed. We started with this task and kept at it daily, our nights were spent in feeding ourselves with eggs and Bass beer, which we could obtain from nearby canteens. Our Major had goal posts put up behind the guns for our football matches, altogether we had rather a good time. Our task of making the emplacement was finished after about a fortnight's work, it was a neat little place, hardly noticeable and many a happy night we Signallers had in our tent. We would get ourselves ready for bed and sit up with our clothes off, a petrol tin fire in the centre with about a dozen candles burning, then a mouth organ would be going with all of us singing to our hearts content. Rum rations were issued, along with the beer we had and we made merry until sleep overtook us. Although I had six different wires running into my telephone exchange, I never had anyone on duty after 11pm, as there was really nothing to do, although it was against regulations, I took the risk of punishment. The eventful evening of 20th March 1918 arrived, on this particular night at about 9.30pm, we Signallers were sitting around our petrol tin fire, we were all talking when the telephone just above my bed, started to buzz. This was unusual for night time, causing everyone to look towards me when I took hold of the receiver. All talking stopped, I put the receiver to my ear and said "Hello", is that "A" Battery? said a voice, "A" Battery Speaking" I replied, "Brigade Major to speak to your O.C." said the voice. I immediately got our O.C. on the phone and told him that the Brigade Major wished to speak to him, then I connected them on my exchange. I kept my telephone receiver to my ear and listened to the conversation, "Hello is that you Major?", "Yes" replied our O.C., then the Brigade Major continued to say "Well, the Bosch will attack about 4.30am tomorrow, please take the necessary precautions, Good night". Our O.C. then said "Good night", I hung the telephone receiver up again and looked at my Signallers sitting up in bed, they were all waiting for me to tell them what had been said. I repeated the exact words, one got up out of bed, then another, until everyone was fully dressed, "Where's my water bottle and haversack"? were the expressions. Everyone was preparing for a quick removal, why, it just seemed to be the general impression that we would have to run for it. The Major rang and told me to give strict attention to the phone during the night. I arranged for my Signallers to have allotted times, each man did his turn of duty on the phone between then and the following morning, I also arranged for it to be my time when the attack was to take place. The NCO in charge of the Guards on guns was instructed to call the Officers and Sergeants at 3.30am, so that all hands would be at their posts when the attack came. The night wore on slowly, some men were sleeping, but the majority were awake, Gunners kept popping into our tent, asking for information. We couldn't tell them anymore than they already knew, namely that the Germans were going to attack at 4.30am, some wouldn't believe it, others half believed it and some ridiculed the idea. Such were the various beliefs of the information, which was now general news throughout the Battery. Midnight came and passed, 1am and 2am came and went, not a sound could be heard, the night was deathly quiet and by 3am everyone was up and ready. I sat on the telephone smoking and my eyes were continually on the little pointers of our watch that was hanging on a matchstick stuck into the clay on the side of the bank. The time moved to 4am, 4.15am, we all watched that large pointer now, 4.20am, 4.25am and still not a sound. That pointer went on – tick, by tick, 4.28am still deathly quiet, 4.29½am, still no sound and then 4.30am, the pointer was dead on the half hour mark, then rumble, rumble, crash, crash, the whole atmosphere shook, the noise was awful, shells could be heard rumbling overhead like aeroplanes. Flashes could be seen in the sky as the shells burst, the noise was like a thousand thunders rolled into one. I tried all my wires, but couldn't get an answer. Our Major came to me and asked if I could get Headquarters, I told him all my wires were broken somewhere and asked him if I should get some men to mend them. He said it would be useless and gave me orders to prepare everything to be ready for a quick departure. Daylight came on 21st March 1918 and we were all hanging about, the Major was walking about his guns, which now had the camouflage taken off. The Gunners were standing by them and the Major kept biting his fingernails with worry. As the day wore on, we saw crowds of our Infantry passing along the main road, which passed on the right of our guns, some were wounded and others just seemed to be stragglers. Then heavy guns kept passing by to the rear, Infantry wagons and baggage carts were amongst a general stream of traffic. Matters weren't rosy, the crossroads to the rear of our guns were being heavily shelled by Fritz's 5.9 shells that were causing awful damage to both horses and men. Large German shells were continuously going overhead to the rear and still we were doing nothing. The bombardment, which started at 4.30am, was still to be heard, but not so intense. Afternoon came and our Major ordered our gun and wagon teams to come up from the rear in close proximity to the guns. At about 5pm, our Major received orders to fire and the Gunners were pleased to help. They rattled the shells off with a good heart, but it only lasted about half an hour, night set in and matters were much quieter. Intermittent gunfire could be heard from Fritz and a few heavies seemed to be firing on our side. He continuously kept shelling the crossroads behind our guns throughout the night, every three minutes or so with 5.9 x 8 inch shells. All night we could hear the steady rumble of all forms of transport passing by our guns on the roadway. Shells from Fritz kept sailing overhead like the noise of railway goods trains travelling at night when everything else was quiet. These shells were meant for roadways and camps right behind our lines. None of us slept that night, everyone being far too jumpy. Our Major was in a very nervous state, not from fear "Oh no", I think that his responsibility for men and guns were what was worrying him. There was also the absence of orders and instructions that added to his responsibility. Dawn came on the second day, the 22nd March and with it an increase of shelling from Fritz. As the guns got out, his aeroplanes made their unwelcome appearance overhead, they were flying very low and would immediately machine gun any man or form of transport they came across. There was a complete absence of anti-aircraft guns on our side and consequently, the aeroplanes did exactly what they liked, no doubt there were various Lewis Gun emplacements rigged up at battery and wagon lines etc., but they had no effect. Our Major asked me to go forward with a companion to try and find out about our Infantry and Fritz's whereabouts. I set off with one of my Signallers across the main road, which was heavily clad with guns and all manner of transport and Infantry. It just seemed to me that all men who had been up at the Front lines were "chucking the sponge up" and going home. After crossing the wood, we got onto high ground and when we gazed in front, we were annoyed to see our Infantry retreating in an orderly manner. They were running across ground then pulling down, facing back to Fritz and letting go a few rounds from their machine guns etc. What met our view most was the Germans, they were walking across the fields in extended order with rifles at the ready, bayonets fixed and they kept lying down as they approached our Infantry letting off bursts of rifle fire. It was a glorious sight, if it hadn't been the seriousness that was attached to it all. On seeing this, we ran as fast as our legs could carry us, back to our guns and told our Major what we had seen. He sent an Officer back with us immediately to take bearings of the situation, then we ran back again. After a brief consultation with our Major and Officer and a hasty reference to maps etc., our Major gave the guns their orders. When the Gunner completed those orders, our guns, instead of pointing directly in front, were switched around half way. The major gave range of a thousand yards or so, then ordered immediate gunfire with high explosive 106 fuse. To see those Gunners work, was a sight to make one proud to be an Englishman. We Signallers kept bringing shells to them, with the Gunners in their shirtsleeves sweating for all they were worth. They got rid of hundreds of shells in a short time and no doubt they would do great damage. During this, the Major had sent the Officer back again to see any fresh developments in our immediate vicinity. He came to me and asked if I could get any information about the way things were going, I could well understand the Major's state of mind. There were the Germans in close proximity, barely a thousand yards away on our right, German aeroplanes flying overhead and doing what they liked, with no planes of ours to be seen. Our Infantry were trooping back to the rear in droves, with everything pointing to a defeat. Poor fellow, I was very sorry for him and we all understood the seriousness. I told him that I knew of a Burnett Cable Test Box[67] about a hundred yards to the rear of the crossroads, he told me to go and get in touch with somebody in authority, so I went taking a Signaller and telephone with me. We ran as fast as we could and when we neared the crossroads, Fritz was shelling very heavily. There were dead men, horses, broken guns

67 A locally made test set which tested line.

and carts, all lying in a mangled mass with shells still dropping amongst that horrible mess. Naturally, we avoided these crossroads by going over an old manure heap, we were nearly suffocated by the stench. We reached the test box, which was a small dugout with the ends of about 50 buried telephone cables fastened to a wooden board, with terminals attached inside. There were no distinguishing marks on any terminal to where each wire was connected, I had to start at one end, fix my phone in and work along each set of two terminals until I received an answer to my buzzing telephone. I tried a matter of twenty with feverish haste, without any luck, and then at last we heard some response to our repeated calling on our telephone buzzer. I had fused my wires onto two terminals and as soon as I put my receiver to my ear, I heard voices, I listened to find out who they were, but to no avail, then I started to buzz my telephone as hard as I could. I stopped and listened and was greeted with "Get off the bloody line", I repeated "Hello, Hello, Hello, this is important, will you listen to me", still I was told to get off the bloody line by a very agitated voice. I wasn't going to give up, then eventually I was asked, "What are you buzzing at? Who are you? Where do you belong"? The extreme agitation in the tone of his voice was very marked indeed. "I want some information" I repeated "and I don't want to say who, or where I am". I had thoughts of German spies using the phones, so I refrained from using the Battery's name etc. Eventually, I mentioned our Major's name and the voice on the other end spoke in tones of agitated relief, "You belong to Col. Higginbottom[68] don't you?" he asked, then he repeated the Colonel's name, I said "Yes", then he said "I'm Brigade Major, take this message quickly and get it to your O.C. at once". Then followed a detailed message of the position of the German Line, what they had captured and where our Line was. There were also various map references telling our guns where to fire, then the Brigade Major finished off with "Don't leave that phone until I tell you", "Right" I

68 It is encouraging to see George knew the name of his CO and spelt the name correctly.

said and sent my Signaller back with the message to our Major. I sat by the phone waiting for any message that might come. My Signaller was coming across to the Test Box again when the words came to me "Hello, Hello", "Yes", I replied, "Take this down at once and get it to your Major without delay". The message was "Retire immediately to Map Reference so and so", signed Brigade Major, and then goodbye. I snapped my wires off the test board, then two of us hooked it as fast as our legs could go. We arrived breathless at our silent guns, with Gunners standing around, empty shell cases scattered all over. Our Major saw us coming and approached with an anxious expression on his face "What is it?" he said excitedly, I handed him the message and he gave the order to ceasefire and prepare to retire. I was told to get the horses, gun and wagon teams, so I signalled to the teams who were a hundred yards away behind a clump of trees, then they came galloping. I told my Signallers to pack up their allotted equipment and get away as fast as they could. I was busy picking up a telephone and other valuable instruments, such as angle of sight, micrometers etc., when the sound of low flying aeroplanes stopped me. I looked up and was horrified to see four German planes swooping around our guns, which were busy limbering up. They started firing their machine guns every time they swooped down towards us. Our "B" or second Battery which was in position just in front of us was being heavily shelled with 8 inch shells and I was nearly stuck to the spot when I saw two 8 inch shells drop right on top of a team of six horses, three drivers and attendant Gunners. When the black smoke cleared away, there was a mass of broken bodies, men and horses lying everywhere. The remainder of that "B" Battery was galloping away up the road. Whether any of those men survived, I cannot say, as just then 8 inch shells started to drop amongst our remaining three guns. No doubt the German planes, which were swooping around, were responsible for all this, as they could see what was going on, they were passing the information back by wireless to their German Heavy Batteries. All my Signallers had gone off, but myself and Jack

Armstrong were on our way when we noticed two of the three guns had got clear away without any casualties. What stopped us was the last gun, this had been on the left flank of the Battery and was separated from its neighbour by a broad deep ditch. It was while trying to get across this ditch that one of the wheel horses had fallen down and we made our way across to where the gun was to help. When we reached the gun, the Gunners were still in shirtsleeves, exerting their strength at the wheels. The drivers, who were on horseback, were flogging the poor beasts for all they were worth. The horse that caused the trouble by falling down had regained its feet and was struggling along with the others. The Sergeant in charge of this gun was doing his utmost to get it out of the ditch and off to safety. Our C.O. and another Officer were giving orders about when to whip the horses and re-group. During all this, German aeroplanes were overhead alternately swooping down towards us and letting off bursts of machine gunfire. 8 inch German shells were dropping all around the vicinity, getting dangerously close to us all. Everyone was in a state of nervous excitement. Eventually, with the combined effort of men and horses, the gun was pulled out of the ditch, then drivers were whipping their horses to gallop away. The Sergeant of the gun had one foot in the stirrup iron of the saddle and was about to get on his horse when an 8 inch shell dropped within a few yards of him. When the smoke cleared, two others and I rushed to the poor fellow who was lying on the ground in agony. The Sergeant was badly wounded on the lower part of his back and as far as I could see, part of the seat of his trousers was blown off. The CO halted the gun when he saw what had happened, then we lifted the Sergeant onto the gun limber, two Gunners got up to hold him on and the gun started to move away. Noticing that we were about to be left behind. Jack Armstrong and I made a grab at the barrel of the gun to get onto it and away. When we did get hold of the gun barrel, we had to let go, as the iron was so hot and the gun was bumping over broken ground, we couldn't get onto it, therefore we had to run or walk. As we went along, we were amazed to see the Germans only a few hundred yards away bullets were hissing past us like bees and we were very anxious. We passed our cookhouse and noticed that the fire was burning merrily with our dinner of six Dixie's of stew, we didn't turn to find out if it was cooked or not. Oh no, "Safety first". We were the last two people to leave the position. When we got to the road, we saw our guns, gauging the time to dash over the crossroads between shells dropping We didn't go the same way, because of the danger of being hit, so we cut across the manure heaps onto the main road and eventually caught up with the guns. When we reached them, I asked about the Sergeant who had been badly wounded, they said he had died and been left on the side of the road, which was clad with all forms of military traffic, mainly guns It just seemed everybody was going away. We travelled about a mile, and then branched off the road into a field, where there was a copse of trees. I was behind this copse, when our O.C. started to put his guns into position once more. Posts were being set up, when about six German Aeroplanes came over and with the sun shining brightly they saw all our movements. They flew around us once and made off, but they hadn't been gone more than two minutes, when there was a roar and a crash. There, right into the copse of trees, dropped two high velocity shells from Fritz. Those aeroplanes had done the trick once again. Our O.C. didn't wait for a second warning and our horses were harnessed to the guns in very quick time. Off we went into the main road at a gallop and on looking around we saw about four high velocity shells drop where our guns had been, remarkable shooting on the part of Fritz. We travelled along the roads until dusk, where we were I couldn't say, as I had lost all understanding regarding the countryside that I knew from maps. We stopped at the roadside and had our second meal of the day, bully and biscuits with water from the ditch. We didn't stay long and moved off once more. We hadn't travelled far before we pulled into a country lane and the guns were placed into position. After some map consulting by our OC, our guns fired the shells we had. Where we were firing to and why, I couldn't say, but it didn't last long and as soon as it was over, we were on the march again. By now it was a moonlit night and everything was quiet, the traffic had disappeared from the roads, and we never came across anybody else that night. We halted on the road, which was very hilly, to give our horses a rest and to keep ourselves awake.

There was a large house standing back from the road, we passed into the front garden and up to the door, then knocked, but got no answer. All was deathly still in the moonlight. We tried the shuttered windows, but still no response. Four of us then went around to the back door, which we thought would be fastened, like the front, but when I gave it a push, my heart nearly stopped when the door opened. Dense blackness met our eyes, with warm air gushing into our faces. We stood at the door and somehow seemed to sense that human beings were in there, and then an uneasy feeling came over us. We lit matches and went into the house with our nerves tight. In the faint glimmer of those matches we couldn't see anything at first, except the usual household furniture. Then someone produced the inevitable candle and we were amazed to see two very old women sitting huddled close to a stove in the middle of the room. We approached them and spoke in French as best we could, but they only gazed at us without saying anything. They carried on doing their job, with their laps full of thin twigs, then each one would break them into small pieces about the length of two matchsticks. Then they put them into the small hole in the top of the stove, where we saw a small glow from the fire that they were trying to keep going. The whole scene was tragic and pitiful. We tried again and again to get them to speak, but it was useless. We eventually left, quietly closing the door after us. The whole thing put us into a despondent mood for the rest of the night.

Eventually dawn broke on the fourth day and we were still on the move. Our ammunition wagons met us during the day, when we had our gun limber restocked with shells. We also did a good deal of firing that day at various positions, the most strenuous being at

Ham and Nesle where we did heavy firing. Only giving up when our ammunition ran out or Fritz got too near for the safety of our guns. During these anxious times we had irregular meals and when we had them, it was the usual hard tack of bully beef and biscuits, with drinking water obtained from streams or ditches. We didn't have time to wash or shave and nearly everyone had no kit because it was either lost or thrown away on account of hasty retreats. The majority of us didn't have blankets to cover ourselves, during daytime it was warm and sunny, but at night it turned cold and frosty. On the evening of the fourth day, we pulled off the main road into a field, placed our guns into position, covered them with branches and bushes as a form of camouflage. Our O.C. told us to get some sleep when we got a chance, we were all flagged out and didn't take much telling. The three of us lay down together for warmth, with only one overcoat to cover us and soon fell asleep, but quickly woke up again with our feet being nearly frozen. When we got up we saw the shape of our bodies on the grass, with the surrounding area uneven with frost, sleep was out of the question without sufficient covering. The majority of us were walking about aimlessly to keep ourselves awake and warm, then suddenly the quiet night atmosphere was broken by the sound of a horse's hooves thudding on the hard main road The sound of the horses galloping drew nearer and nearer, everyone's eyes were turned towards the roadway, then the noise ceased as suddenly as it had started. Then we heard a horse thudding across the field towards us. At last the horseman loomed up in the shadows, dismounted and asked for our O.C., then gave him a message. On reading this, our O.C. immediately gave orders to limber up the guns and prepare to move. As each gun was ready, it had to immediately move onto the main road. In the space of quarter of an hour every gun and wagon was moved our Officer rode along the line of guns and told every dismounted man to get on the guns or wagons as best they could, as those who didn't would be left behind. The Officers told us that the German Cavalry had broken through and we had to hook it quick.

We Gunners and Signaller's were soon onto the guns and wagons, with some getting on horseback. We started walking at first then cantering and eventually galloping. The whole Battery went very fast along the moonlit roads, turning corners, practically on two wheels. I was sitting astride the gun barrel facing the horses and what a task I had to keep on. This mad gallop lasted for nearly half an hour then we slowed down to a walking pace.

Dawn of the fifth day arrived with us still on the march, passing through various deserted villages. Our O.C. came and told us to go into the various Estaminets and help ourselves because the Germans would do it, so we might as well have first pick. When we got back to the Battery, all the empty shell baskets in the gun and wagon limbers were full of bottles of wine and beer etc. A most wonderful sight then met our eyes, a proper Godsend, for there right in front of us, on the side of the road, was a large ration dump. Army stores of every description were there, bags of bread, cases of Nestles and Ideal milk, sides of beef, everything that was necessary for troops, with not a single person in charge of it. Our O.C. halted the guns, then there was a raid on the dump. Everything that could be loaded onto the guns and wagons was put there and each man had his loaf of bread and various other rations. We started off again along the dusty sunlit road. Nearly every man had a sandwich of bread and Nestles milk, which stuck to our beards, then the dust stuck to the milk. We were in a lovely mess, in fact we all looked like "Golliwogs". We eventually stopped on some high ground and the guns were once more put into position. The cooks soon had fires roaring and the Dixie's were boiling full of meat, pork & beans etc., then in about a couple of hours we all had as much as we could eat. As a surprise to us, our O.C. came around and organised the issue of fags and tobacco, these had been obtained from the ration dump without our knowing, so we had our first real feed and smoke since the 21st March.

I went forward to where the high ground started to dip into the valley, reeled out some thin Japanese black enamel wire and soon had a telephone fixed up between the Battery and my Officer. We tested it all night and then the Officer said to me "Just you watch the white road on the far side of the valley and you'll see Fritz's scouts come along". I looked over to where the Officer pointed and saw a road coming into view from the outskirts of a wood. After visualizing our recent march, I recognized this particular part of roadway as the one we had passed over before we came to the ration dump. My Officer told me that all our guns were laid onto this stretch of roadway and that the Germans must pass along. Any Officer observing a considerable number of them had to give the order to fire "hell for leather style". There we sat, anxiously waiting and hoping that the Germans would at least put in an appearance. Our Gunners were at their posts all anxious to have a smack at Fritz again, but it wasn't to be. We received orders to come in just before dusk and were off on the road again.

Rumours had it that Fritz was encircling us, so we had to be nippy and get away. We passed through major towns of Roye and Montdidier[69] the next day and a welcome sight greeted us on the wide main roads thousands of French troops met us on our way back, Lancers, Infantry and Artillery, all making their way towards the Germans, what a relief it was to us to see so many troops coming to help us. We stopped at the village of Cottenchy on the Somme District and were billeted in a large mansion.

We had a big drawing room for our quarters and made ourselves as comfortable as possible. All the rooms were stocked with everything a house of its size usually had. The bedrooms had their respective beds all laid neat and tidy, our Officers had a bed each and we humped bedding down from the bedrooms to make our sleeping quarters in the drawing room. We were soon scrounging around the outhouses and gardens at the back of the house and were rewarded

69 The route the battery took is clear. It followed the main route now the D930 from St Quentin through Nesle, Roye and Montdidier from there they must have taken the D935 to Amiens and then diverted to the village of Cottenchy where the Chateau was.

for our search, when we found potatoes, turnips and a few cabbages. We then searched the cupboards and drawers and found split peas, flour, cocoa and saccharine. Eventually we had a roaring fire in the grate with boiling pans and when the whole fare was dished out, we had boiled potatoes, turnip, cabbage, bully beef and peas pudding followed by cocoa. During this feast, there was a knock at the door and when we opened it, we saw a tall French Officer with our O.C., they passed complimentary remarks about the neat and tidy manner in which the room was and wished us a good feast. Our O.C. came back later and told us the French Officer had lived in the mansion with his wife and family and came back to have a last look before its inevitable destruction by the Germans. There was a grand piano in the front drawing room where we had a singsong before resting for the night. We all slept sound except those who were on duty at the phones.

On the second day we did a little firing and noticed that two of our 601b batteries were making a position behind the mansion, then they opened fire in the afternoon. After a few rounds from these guns with their ear-splitting bangs, large pieces of plaster from the ceilings started to fall to the floor and window panes would break and crash. After the last shell was fired at the end of the day, the rooms of that lovely mansion were in an awful state. We were pleased with ourselves, to think that the French Officer had come to say goodbye to his home. God only knows what a state he would have been in, if he had come a day later to see the indiscernible confusion in his home.

On the morning of the third day: we were told to prepare to leave, as we were going out of action for a rest. By the afternoon we were on the road once more, feeling rather happy about going out of it for a while. We had proceeded a good distance, when we halted on the road because of dense traffic. The traffic going towards the Germans was still moving slowly, they were all French troops with light and heavy artillery, then the traffic eventually stopped. About four of us were sitting on the trail of the gun watching the passing troops. When they had stopped moving, we noticed the troops opposite us were dressed in a dirty yellow uniform. We started to argue amongst ourselves as to what French Regiment they belonged to and after various names had been put forward, another Signaller and I said we would go and ask one of them. We approached one of these troops, who was sitting on the bank side smoking a fag. When he saw us, he looked and smiled, but didn't speak, we smiled in return, then I asked him this "Vous Foreign Legion M'Seur?", but he still sat smoking and smiling. I repeated the question, but he got up and threw his fag away. We both stood looking at him working out our best French to ask him again, but there was no need as he gave us the surprise of our life. He was standing close to us, with a pleasant smile on his face and said, "Why Ay Man" in a broad Tyneside twang we nearly dropped when we heard our own "doorstep tongue" being spoken by what we thought was a French soldier. We weren't long in falling into our Tyneside language and after a handshake of a hearty style, we took him across the other side of the road and introduced him to all the boys from good old Tyneside. He told us that he was in the French Foreign Legion and before the war in 1913 he had been in the Northumberland Fusiliers, stationed at Newcastle Barracks. From there he had deserted and after various adventures, had enlisted in the Foreign Legion and had just come from Morocco, we nearly shook his hands off. He got every jug we had, lots of bread, even pieces of candles and as both streams of traffic moved off, there were shouts of "Good old Tyneside and Canny Newcastle" then we passed out of each other's view.

We moved off and then we eventually camped and were refitted. We had about 3 weeks to get ourselves "back to normal", and then off we went into action at Englebelmer, a scene of a Wagon Line of ours in 1916. We kept changing our position on this front to Mailly-Maillet, Beaussart & Colincamps.[70] We left Beaussart in August 1918 and proceeded to Boiry,[71] to take part in another offensive.

70 All these villages are behind the old July 1916 Somme positions.
71 Just south of Arras.

Chapter 9

Home Leave 1918

The BEF is now advancing in a NE direction taking up the slack as the Germans withdraw. This is the Hundred Days in which the war in the west is won. The movement was fast as the German Armies collapse in front of French, British and now America Armies. 4th Army was advancing in the Arras to Albert sector and a breakthrough was made on 8th of August. George must have been sad to miss some of the fun. However it should be remembered that the British Army lost 300,000 men in these last days, some of these were part of the influenza epidemic which was beginning to bite in Europe.

We chased Fritz through Moyenville, Hamelincourt[72] and onto the St. Leger Front. Fritz was making a determined stand in the vicinity of Bullecourt, so this necessitated us to dig in to make gun pits and dugouts etc. One gunner had been busy digging for a dugout and had laid down for a rest, with his bare arm resting in the soil he had been digging. He got up and complained of his arm smarting and when he examined it, he found a mass of blisters from wrist to elbow; he had been resting his arm on ground that must have had a mustard

72 All very close to each other and their involvement was part of the 4th Army's attack south of Amiens

gas shell on it, so he was taken to Hospital. My Pal Teddy Watmough and I constructed our little dugout as we had been accustomed to sleeping together whenever the opportunity occurred. My Signallers had rigged up a telephone pit in the bank side, so we sat down at dusk around the inevitable petrol tin fire. Someone shouted "Elder you're wanted", I came out of the telephone pit to see our Major standing there."Oh! Elder" he said. "Your leave has come through so get packed and off you go at once". I was overjoyed and started to tremble at the thought of it and it didn't take me long to get my kit together. I went to my Pal Teddy Watmough, held out my hand and said "Well. Ta Ta Ted". He said "Geordie, there's something going to happen to me here". "Oh shut up man, don't be daft" I replied, "You'll be here all right when I come back", "Oh well Geordie, I feel it" he said. After bucking him up as best I could, I promised to go and visit his mother when I got home. I then walked about 10 kilometres to the Station at Boyelles[73], where I boarded a train of cattle trucks going to Boulogne. Two days later, I stepped off the train at Newcastle at 11 pm and was soon in the arms of my wife and kiddies. The following day I was walking through the streets of Newcastle with my wife, when I saw one of our Headquarters' Signallers coming towards us, we met and shook hands. "Hello Geordie" he said, "Did you hear about Teddy", I nearly dropped at those words, my wife took hold of my arm and asked me what was wrong. Those words of my pal Ted Watmough immediately flashed through my brain. "Geordie, there's something going to happen to me". Then the Headquarters' Signaller told me the same night that I left my Battery, Teddy and a Driver who took my place, had been literally blown to pieces by an 8 inch German shell that dropped on top of the dugout. Poor Ted, he must have known, a finer lad one couldn't find. I was sick and faint with the shock of the news. I could no more visit my pal's mother than I could fly. He was uppermost in my thoughts all my fortnight at home and when

73 Just forward of where George had left his battery.

my time was up to leave my wife and kiddies, it made me think deeply.[74]

I am not ashamed to say that on the night I left Newcastle Station to go back to France. I was hopelessly drunk. On arriving at Kings Cross, I made up my mind to have three days in London and to hell with Regulations, the passes and all the Army. My feelings in Kings Cross Station at 6.30am were of utter abandonment. I had a hectic time with the money I had left and eventually presented myself at the platform gate in Victoria Station for the train to Folkestone. The difference between the date on my leave Pass and the date I presented myself showed that I was three days over my allotted leave period. Accordingly my Pass was stamped by the RTO and I knew I would be in for trouble when I eventually arrived at my Battery.

The train journey to Folkestone was uneventful, but with a marked contrast between the time a fortnight previous when I was on my way home. Everyone in my compartment seemed to be in no mood for talking, we just sat in our respective places with our thoughts. We eventually arrived at Folkestone and went to the camp on the Front and lounged about until 2pm. We were then marched to the quayside to board the four boats, which were to take us across the Channel to France and the War. I was amongst the last batch to board one of the boats and eventually got on an old Belgian paddle steamer, which was the last to leave the quayside. The other three steamers had already set off and were standing outside the piers waiting until the paddle steamer came out. We started out across the Channel, the four steamers forming a square, with the attendant Destroyers and Battleships surrounding us, "Full speed ahead" was the order and we were soon travelling at a fast pace. Feeling miserable, tired and weary, I went below to lie down by the side of the steamer. The hum of the engines and swish of water lulled me off into a semi-stupor. I couldn't

74 Bombardier E Watmough of A Battery 315 Bde RFA was killed on 31 August 1918. He was 27 years old and was one of three brothers all of whom died in the war. He is buried at Achiet-Le-Grand Communal Cemetery Extension, just behind the locations where George had just left for his leave.

say how long I was in this state. I woke up with a start, feeling very much worse than before and realised it must have been the silence of the engines that woke me. Everyone was making for the deck. I was under the impression we had arrived at Boulogne. When I reached the deck, I saw two piers in the distance and thought we must have made a quick crossing. I could see nothing of the other 3 steamers, so concluded that they must have already entered Boulogne Harbour. I then observed a destroyer coming towards us at full speed from the seaward direction, with its boughs cutting the water like a knife. As it passed us on the portside, I noticed a Naval Signaller calling up with a couple of small signalling flags. Being a Signaller, I immediately concentrated on the flags and read the message which the destroyer was sending to our steamer, "Return to Folkestone at 6 knots". then it turned around and set off to sea at full speed. I asked a Sergeant standing by me "So we are going back to Folkestone again are we?" He looked at me, laughed heartily and said "Well, man, we haven't left yet, there are the piers over there". It transpired that our paddle steamer's engine had partly broken down and couldn't keep up with the other three who went across the Channel without us. Therefore the destroyer had returned to give our Captain orders to return to Folkestone, none of us were sorry about returning and I realised I had only slept for about half an hour. We eventually pulled alongside Folkestone Pier and were soon back at camp again.

The time was 4pm and tea was dished up, then after it was over, the troops wandered aimlessly around the enclosed grounds. Every now and again a crowd of about fifty men would approach the guards, trying to persuade them to let them out into the town, but to no avail. At about 6pm the crowds had increased enormously at the gates, all clamouring to be let out. Eventually, the Camp Commander was sent for and after he had given all those present a severe lecture about being respectable and soldier-like, he said everyone could leave, but must be back by 11 pm. There was a hearty cheer from the troops, the gates were open and we all rushed out onto the streets of Folkestone like a lot of children coming out of school. When I went into Folkestone, I had twenty five shillings so I was determined to have a jolly last night on my own. I went to the first Public House I saw, asked for a pint and was greeted with "Sorry, Sir: we don't serve men in Uniform" The whole joy of getting out of camp for this last night in England was completely taken from me There was nothing else to do, but wander about like sheep. I waited until the last possible minute before I re-entered the camp and went to bed. We were all up early and marched to the steamer at about 9.30am, with another group of men who had returned from London that morning. This time, the old paddle steamer had been left out. We made an uneventful crossing and were soon on our way up the hill to St. Martins Camp at Boulogne, where I remained for 3 days. I was then sent to Arras Station to ask where my Battery was. When I arrived at Arras, I saw the RTO and he told me he hadn't any news of my Battery's whereabouts. I wasn't the least perturbed, as it meant more days away from the horrors of war, but I had my leave Pass to think about, with its three days over-stayed leave conspicuously visible. I had a plan to counteract this evidence, which I knew would get me into trouble when I eventually arrived back at my Battery. When the RTO gave me the information regarding my Battery, I asked him to stamp my Pass, as proof of enquiring about my Battery and he sent me to his Clerk. I handed my Pass over positioning it in such a manner that when he stamped the date and district, it covered the date that was entered at Victoria Station in London. The RTO then told me to go a couple of miles up to the rail head and ration dump, as they might have news of my Battery's whereabouts.

Having jumped various motor Lorries, I eventually arrived at the railhead and was told that my Unit was in this vicinity, but they didn't know which district. My main worry was to get my Pass stamped, so I asked the Officer in charge to do it, thus adding another District stamp. I asked for rations and a place to stop for the night and was put into a little tin shed amongst many sacks of corn I soon made myself comfortable, then after having something to eat I went to sleep. Next morning I was up early and went to the Officer to see it he could tell me where to find my Unit. He said he had no idea, but he would look through files of various Units to see if he could trace them. Whilst he was doing this, a Sergeant who was in attendance told us he had been to that Unit near Bapaume, with hay about a fortnight ago. Before I left, I had the date stamped on my Pass.

There were no trains to Bapaume at this time, because the rails were out of order, so I had to use my wits to get over those many intervening miles. It took 2 days to get there, mainly by motor lorry and walking. When I eventually reached Bapaume, my Pass was a mess of stamps from different RTO's, the only date which was distinguishable was the start of my leave period. The rest of the Pass was a mass of blue and black stamping ink with various letters intermixed and I viewed my Pass with a smile of satisfaction, knowing it was a job well done. At Bapaume I was told that my Battery was on the banks of the Canal-Du-Nord some eight kilometres away. It was whilst standing at a YMCA hut getting a pot of cocoa and a packet of biscuits, that I came across one of our drivers who had left the Battery to get canteen supplies, so off I went to join them. Having arrived, I went to the Officer's tent and was greeted with "Hello Elder, just got back?", "Yes, Sir" I replied, "I had an awful job finding the Battery Sir" I said "So did I" he replied. "I've just got back myself from leave" "That'll do Elder, just report to your sub-section and by the way, have you got your Pass?" I fumbled in my pockets and handed it to him, he looked, smiled and said "all right". As I left his tent, I thought I saw him wink his eye as he held the Pass. I was soon made comfortable in a "Bivi" belonging to one of my sub-section and spent the night there.

Next morning I was doing ordinary stable duties and at about 7.30am, I heard the Battery Orderly shout my name, I knew what it was for before I saw him, I was to go to the gun position. True enough, I was to report to the Sergeant in charge of the gunpoint. At about 10pm I left the Wagon Line then proceeded to the guns, the locality was a total mystery in the darkness. Things were very quiet and I groped my way across broken ground to the Major's dugout. I arrived and was told the direction of the Signallers dugout and told to take charge forthwith. After a good deal of stumbling about and falling into shell holes, I eventually arrived at the Signallers dugout. On entering I was struck with a lot of strange faces, there were four Signallers who were old hands of the Battery but the others were all strangers. Having asked where the others were, I was told all had died, some badly gassed and others under the ground in the St. Leger - Bullecourt Sector. This news absolutely flattened my spirit, or what was left of it, it seemed to cast a gloom over everything. Of all of the boys I had trained and had merry nights with since joining up in 1915, there were only four Signallers and me left. It just disheartened one beyond explanation.

Chapter 10

The Hindenburg Line and Wounded 1918

In September 1916 Hindenburg was the German Chief of Staff with Ludendorff as his First Quartermaster General. This marked a change in strategy and one of the decisions made was the building of a new defensive line well behind the existing German line in 1916. We know already how effective German fortifications were and so they became on this Hindenburg Line as it was called. After the Hundred Days following the German March offensive the Germans had by and large pulled back to the Hindenburg Line and if the war was to be brought to a close this line had to be breached by the Allies. Haig resolved to attack in September 1918. The lead up to the battle from August to 26 September had already cost the British 180,000 casualties so the final struggle was likely to be costly and this was a major concern both in France and at home. George's following account deals with the battles surrounding the actual breaking of the Hindenburg line which in the end took only 8 days. George's battery would have been supporting the 4th Army as it advanced towards Cambrai and Mons the towns where it all started. But during this period George is wounded and he is out of it for a bit. His account of being received into hospital is revealing and what is also noteworthy is his almost complete disdain for victory or the Armistice.

Morning arrived and with it an attack of our Infantry with a heavy barrage, this lasted well into the morning and all afternoon our guns were silent. Large numbers of our aeroplanes kept going overhead towards Fritz's lines. We were told by one Officer that Fritz had hooked it, so at night we pulled out our guns and proceeded to the Wagon Line. On the following day we left and went back by way of Bapaume and Peronne, cutting right across the old battlefields of 1915-16-17. A more horrible scene of desolation and ruin one couldn't wish to see. Eventually on about 24th September 1918, we took up position on the Cambrai Front. The next morning, we were arranging a barrage fire that lasted all day so everyone was very tired, but no rest for the troops who were on the offensive. All that night we heard heavy guns getting into position behind us and the news filtered through that another big attack was to take place at dawn; therefore no one had any rest.

About half an hour before dawn, our Officer came around to see if everything was in order and at the pre-arranged time, all our guns opened out a murderous bombardment on Fritz's lines. The whole countryside was lit up with gun flashes and trench lights. The noise of bursting shells from Fritz's guns and the reports of our small and heavy guns added to the din, the noise was awful, so one had to shout to be heard. Gradually the light crept into the Heavens, then soon after out came the sun shining its warm rays on what must have been an awful carnage of human beings. Our Battery gradually increased their range until they were firing at the furthest range possible for an 18lb gun, then the ceasefire came along giving us a rest. We were told Fritz had been pushed back out of range altogether.

After an hour or two, horses came up from the horse lines for the Officers and I was told that I had to mount also. I was soon on a horse. And on my back was a large wooden board about two feet square which held an Artillery Map of the district, I also had a telephone and a couple of signalling flags. After all the Officers and attendant horse holders had mounted, we all set off in a forward direction. We hadn't gone far before we met another body of mounted men, consisting of our Colonel, Headquarters Officers, Signallers, Officers and attendant Horse holders from our "B" "C" and "D" Batteries. After each Battery O.C. had conversed with the Colonel, we all set off with the Colonel in front. We were all walking our horses over the various batches of barbed wire and shell holed ground, looking like a troop of cavalry. As we went along, I observed and remarked to a horse holder that Fritz had only one observation Balloon up in the air and that we would get it in consequence. I had no sooner said this to my companion when there was a screech, a hiss and a terrible explosion to the left of us, then in quick succession, two more explosions, which were followed by another four. The whole lots of shells were dropped all around us and the Colonel, realising the danger to men and horses, immediately gave the order to gallop and scatter. This was in quick time, which was a Godsend, as salvo after salvo of four shells at a time came over from Fritz at lightning speed. There we were, galloping for all we were worth scattered in a forward direction, with our horses jumping like acrobats, over bundles of barbed wire and large shell holes. This mad ride only lasted about five minutes, but it was necessary, luckily no one was hit. We all met further down the hillside and after resting our horses we pushed on again, passing through a breach in the walls of the empty Canal-Du-Nord. We then dismounted in a sunken road. Our Colonel and C.O.'s had another talk and each Battery Commander then went off in a different direction, with his attendant staff.

My Officer and I clambered up the sides of the sunken road into a field of green grass, then walked up the hill. The sun was shining and with the absence of either gun or rifle fire, it seemed like a summer outing in the country. We approached the top of the hill and as we got on higher ground, we could see more of the countryside that lay directly in front of us, with the houses of Cambrai in the distance.

My Officer stopped to check the position on the map, which was still strapped onto my back. There we were, right on top of a crest of a hill in full view of our enemy, although we didn't know his exact position. The white map and board must have been an easy target in the brilliant sunshine to any eyes that might be watching. My Officer looked through his binoculars towards Cambrai, with a view to picking a new position for our guns. We had to get a fairly decent estimate of Fritz's present Front Line and hadn't much time to waste. My Officer asked me if I could see anything of our guns, I looked back and saw nothing, although there were plenty of our Infantry marching forward. Suddenly there was a rattle of machine gun fire about fifty yards away, with bullets scattering up the turf all around us. We both immediately dropped flat onto the floor on our stomachs, then the firing stopped My Officer then said "Come on Elder, there's a bit of high ground in front, it'll be more cover for us", then he got up, ran forward and I followed close to his heels We hadn't gone 6 yards, when the firing started again, then suddenly my right foot received a terrible blow that knocked my leg away from under me. I fell to the ground, coming out with the most awful curses a man could utter. If I could have gotten hold of that German at that moment, I would have ripped him open from ear to ear, such were my feelings in the moment of agony from the bullet. My Officer ran back to me at imminent risk to himself, with the machine gun giving spasmodic bursts of fire. I lay on my back to keep out of sight of the machine gunners, as it was quite evident we had been seen and they were watching for any movement. My Officer lay between my feet and took my boot off by cutting the laces, it was covered with blood. On examining it, I found two clear holes where the bullet had entered at the fourth lace hole, cut a groove through the top of my foot and out the other side. Lucky for me it hadn't penetrated deeper, the small vein on the top of the foot burst and a great deal of blood was lost. My Officer took his first aid dressing and applied the iodine to bandage my foot, but the blood started to ooze through it. I then gave him my dressing to put on and my foot was quite numb by this time. My Officer asked if I was all right and I said, as well as could be expected. He told me he would like to take me to a dressing station, but he had his duty to do, so couldn't. I said I would manage, he shook my hand wished me the best of luck, got up with my map board and telephone and left.

I thought it was madness to remain where I was, so I sat up and no sooner said than done, I was greeted with several bursts of machine gun bullets which cut up the turf in the immediate vicinity. I very quickly lay on my back again, then saw our Infantry coming up the slope and they started to entrench themselves as best they could. I was laying right in line with them, then several saw me and shouted, "Are you all right chum?" As far as I could see our Infantry were digging in along the hilltop just below the skyline. Fritz then started to send over a few high velocity shells. As they were dropping uncomfortably close to me I made a further endeavour to crawl away down the slope, as I knew it would be dangerous for me to raise my body up I turned over on my stomach, even this small movement brought another burst of machine gun bullets into my vicinity. As a last resort, I made levers of my elbows, sticking them into the turf and exerting all my strength to pull my body along. I managed to get further down the hillside and out of observation. I made an effort to stand up, but could only do so on my left leg, as my right leg was causing me terrible pain. I was in agony when I touched the ground and all I could do was hop until I got to the sunken road where we left our horses, but they weren't there,

For once, luck came my way along this road were great streams of guns, Infantry transport of every description, all making their way to fresh positions, so they could harass Mr. Fritz. Suddenly, amongst the throng, I spotted one of our gun limbers making their way over to the rear. I shouted to them, they came over, lifted me onto the limber and we galloped towards the crossing over the Canal-Du-Nord. As we approached, we saw that Fritz was shelling the crossing; great black shells were dropping near to each side of the Canal, with our traffic making dangerous dashes to get across. We stopped a good distance away because of the traffic control troops, who were controlling the amount of traffic that made a dash across the Canal. On the opposite side of the Canal, I saw a gun and six horses galloping, with the gun rolling from side to side behind them. They came to the centre of the crossing, and then there was a gurgle and a rush through the air of about four of Fritz's heavy shells, which dropped right in front of the gun. The whole crossing was clouded in thick black smoke and we thought the drivers and horses had been blown to bits, but out of the thick black smoke they came, like something emerging from beyond. Still at a mad gallop they came, eventually stopping a few yards away from us and true to the tradition of the Artillery Drivers, they dismounted, and then ran their hands over every part of their horses' bodies to check if they had been hit, their first thoughts were for their faithful mounts.

Then came our turn to get across, so off we went at a gallop. Mad ride wasn't the exact description it seemed the most difficult task ever to keep on the Gun Limber seat. Several times when one of the wheels dropped into a shell hole for when the drivers drove their horses at a trench and the Gun Limber jumped over, I nearly fell off, eventually getting across without anything happening, going on our way at a trot.

It was at about this time, that I wrote a Field Post Card to my wife, to tell her I was in Hospital and feeling well. Owing to the jostling of the Gun Limber I was sitting on, the writing on the card was very shaky and straggling. I learned afterwards from my wife that everyone at home judged my wounded condition from the state of the writing and were very concerned, until I wrote and told them I was O.K.

I left the Gun Limber because they had to go in a different direction and had to hobble along for two kilometres before I reached the Aid Post[75]. When I eventually arrived, there was a long string of

75 Although George does not mention the location of the Field Hospital it was

wounded about six deep, all waiting for attention. I took my place in line and waited patiently even though I felt faint due to heavy blood loss and over excitement. Men were dropping down every minute from weakness and pain from their wounds. RAMC men would patrol the line looking for the more serious cases, then rush them to the Front. Church and Salvation Army men came along giving us fags and tea with above all, a cheerful word, which though simple and commonplace, gave the wounded a lot of comfort.

Slowly but surely, the line moved up to the large tent where the Doctors were giving first aid. As each man entered the tent in single file, so the line of wounded moved slowly towards the Doctors at the far end of the tent. RAMC men were there, giving each wounded man instructions to open their tunics and shirt to bare their chests. Further on, another RAMC man was standing with an enamel basin and a brush soaked in iodine. As each man approached him, he would drop the brush into the basin, then make a large circle on the wounded's left breast. Having done this, each man moved along still further to where two Doctors were standing at a small table The Doctor would nip the flesh of the wounded man's left breast between his forefinger and thumb, then inoculate with a large needle and syringe. After this was performed, each man then passed into the real dressing department. Here, Doctors would examine each man's wound, then give the necessary instructions to those responsible for dressing the wounds. They would also decide who was a stretcher case or able to walk. Each man had a card attached to his tunic button, which held his particulars. After dressing, each man went to the waiting room tent. Stretcher cases were first and others, when possible, were loaded into RAMC Red Cross Motors then as each car was full it went at full speed back to the Hospitals There were eight of us in the motor all classed as walkers. We travelled along roads for a good while, eventually pulling up into a field Red Cross Station, where

---

most likely at Carnieres as he marked this on the map he left with his family. This is just a few miles east of Cambrai.

we were taken to a large tent along with hundreds of others from all parts of the Front.

In the tent were heaps of buttered bread, jars of various jams, large tins of loose figs and packets of tobacco. Church Army men were walking around with pails of hot tea and cocoa for anyone who wanted it. Each wounded man had every opportunity to satisfy his hunger during his wait in the tent, but the majority of us didn't feel like eating. We eventually left one by one, were examined by the Doctors and had our wounds re-dressed. We were then put into Motors once again, eventually reaching a railway siding where an ambulance train was waiting. This was soon loaded up to full capacity and as darkness came, we set off. I sank into the carriage seat with a feeling of resignation and soon the gentle rumble of the wheels lulled me off to sleep

I eventually reached a Hospital in the town of Camiers[76], near the coast and my first task was to get bathed before I went to bed. The usual Hospital routine was waking up each patient at about 4.00am telling him to get his face and hands washed, woe betide the Tommy who tried to go asleep again, or put the bedclothes over his head. One chap next to me had a small wound in the ball of his right leg and made no secret of wanting to go to England. After one of the Doctors examinations he saw his chances of getting home were very poor,

---

76 Camiers is just South of Boulogne and North of Etaples. There were three hospitals at Camiers, No 20 General, No 22 General and No 42 Stationary. The Base Hospital was part of the casualty evacuation chain, further back from the front line than the Casualty Clearing Stations. They were manned by troops of the Royal Army Medical Corps, with attached Royal Engineers and men of the Army Service Corps. In the theatre of war in France and Flanders, the British hospitals were generally located near the coast. They needed to be close to a railway line, in order for casualties to arrive (although some also came by canal barge); they also needed to be near a port where men could be evacuated for longer-term treatment in Britain. There were two types, known as Stationary and General Hospitals. They were large facilities, often centred on some pre-war buildings such as seaside hotels. The hospitals grew hugely in number and scale throughout the war. Most of the hospitals moved very rarely until the larger movements of the armies in 1918.

because the Doctor thought his wound wasn't serious enough. One night before lights out, he told me he would make sure he would get to "Blighty". I asked him how this was possible; he said "watch me". He then asked for a water bottle from an Orderly, immediately urinated into it then kept it under his bed. After the lights were turned down and the nurses had made everybody comfortable for the night, he brought out the bottle, which was half full of his urine. He then took off the dressings, saturated a large piece of cotton wool covered his wound, then rewound the bandages very tightly. The next morning the Doctor came round to examine each patient's wounds. He went to my mate and asked how he had slept. He told him he hadn't, because of the pain. When the Doctor removed his bandages, I was amazed to see the state of his wound. It was inflamed, angry looking and twice its normal size, with ragged edges. The Doctor said it was serious and immediately marked my mate for "Blighty". The same afternoon, he was taken out of bed, put on a stretcher and then to the Hospital train, which took him to the Docks and then to Blighty.

I fared differently as the Doctor said that I could get out of bed during the day to help on the Ward. This consisted of wheeling around what us Tommie's called the "Agony Table", because it was used by the Doctor and Matron to dress our wounds, on it were various items such as lint, lotions and ointments etc. I was also asked to watch men as they came around from the effects of Chloroform, ensuring they didn't do any damage to their wounds or dressings in their semi-conscious state. One chap had undergone an operation to his right arm and was brought back to bed, his arm was fully extended, pointing upright with a piece of bandage fastened to a hook in the ceiling, holding his right wrist to keep his arm up. I had my work cut out trying to stop him pulling everything away, but I also had several good laughs. While he was gradually coming out of the Chloroform he would say some of the queerest things and language, he must have thought he was after the Germans.

One day, I was lying in bed after breakfast, when an old man who had been taken to the Operating Room the previous night, was brought back to bed. I lay watching him, amused by his expressions and antics and he wasn't long in gaining his senses, laying there intently gazing at his leg. He looked around the Ward then called to a passing Nurse, who went over to him, she said "Now Dad, what do you want?" He looked right into her eyes without speaking then said, "Nurse, if I ask you a question, will you tell me the truth?" "Well Dad" she said "if it is possible for me to answer your question, I will do it truthfully". Then the old man looked at his leg and said "I can move my toes, feel my foot and move my knee", but, then he paused and looked at the Nurse and suddenly he blurted out "Nurse, is my left foot off?" She looked at him with sympathy coming from her eyes and said Yes" and backed slowly away from his bed. "That's all I want to know" he said, looking at his left leg.

On another day I had been wheeling the Agony Table with the Doctors and was quite busy with the last patient, when the Matron said to the Doctor that he might as well examine my foot. My bandages were removed and he poked and squeezed, asking if I felt any pain, I of course said "yes". He said it still had an angry look, then turned to the Matron and said" Shall we send this chap across?" I looked hoping she would say yes, but she said "I don't think so; he can go to the convalescent Camp in a day or two". The effect of those words will live with me to my dying day. I felt as if I could have kicked her until she was in pieces. To think that one of my own countrywomen would spoil a Tommy's chance of getting home to his wife and kiddies, I was full of hatred, such was the mentality the war produced.

I was pleased to be sent away a few days later to a Convalescent Camp[77] at Caen on the coast of the English Channel. Every day, before breakfast, the troops marched along the sands with the Band, the air was splendid and we soon began to feel the benefit. Our food was of

77 A number of Convalescence Camps were established to relieve the Base Hospitals of recovering troops. They were not always a bundle of roses.

a high standard and we had no work to do. There were also a large number of recreations in the camp, so each man could always find something new each day.

We used to get the Paris Edition of the Daily Mail brought to the Camp at 8.00am and what a rush there was for it. Whilst I was at the Camp, I heard that the War had finished, but apart from a few lurid remarks there was nothing abnormal. Everyone seemed to take the finish of the war in a cold way, just a matter of a day's work. I stayed here for about three weeks, then I was sent away with a batch of troops down to the Artillery Base at Le Havre. The journey took about 20 hours in cattle trucks, which were obviously not made for men. The truck I shared with about twenty others, had floor planks with spaces in-between, so one could see the ballast of the railway as the train went along. We left the Camp late in the afternoon and as darkness came upon us, we lay down on the floor to rest, but sleep was impossible owing to the rush of air through the spaces in the floor. At noon on the following day, we eventually reached Le Havre which was really a sub-station called Harfleur and we were glad to get out after each man's particulars had been taken. We were allocated into our respective sections such as RGA. RFA, RHA. and Signallers.

Chapter 11

Riots 1918

The war was over but there was almost immediate disillusionment at the slow pace of repatriation. Men had worked hard for 4 years in many cases, risked their lives and now it was over all they wanted to do was to go home. The Army was nigh on a million men and such things were going to take time. Patience was not on great abundance with the soldiers and frequently there were disturbances. The hierarchy invariably did not play these incidents well. The quality of leadership in these rear areas was always questionable. Perhaps the most well known riots or mutinies were those in 1917 at the "Bull Ring" at Etaples, known by soldiers as "eat apples". George's account is an interesting one and underlines the difficulties that these camps generated.

This Royal Field and Garrison Artillery Base Depot, was full to capacity, huts and tents were dotted all over and adjoining the Artillery Camps were Infantry Depots, Riflemen, Guards and London Scottish etc. Large batches of men were coming into the camps every day. There must have been hundreds of thousands of troops in the two camps. Meal times consisted of three to four sittings, which led to a good deal of trouble having very serious consequences, which is stated as follows:-

RIOTS AT THE R.A. AND R.F.A. BASE DEPOT HARFLEUR LE HAVRE, FRANCE AT 3.30PM ON DECEMBER 9TH 1918

At this stage of the War, there were large numbers of troops quartered here and as one can readily understand, it was a very great task for those in command to arrange the feeding of these large numbers, this was really the origination of the riots.

The first of the trouble started in the dining hut of the RFA Signallers, though there had been a lot of squabbling at the RGA Section on 8th December. On 9th December complaints were made at the midday meal, in regulation manner to the Orderly Officer, on his visit to the dining hut. The potatoes served were very dirty and the meal was insufficient. As I was an NCO in charge of a table and responsible for serving the "grub" in equal portions to about 24 men, I made a complaint along with several other NCO's. On hearing the complaints, the Orderly Officer inspected the food and promised to investigate and inform us of the result. With that he left and didn't return. After a good deal of chatter amongst the troops and rattling of dinner plates on the tables, it all passed over.

The next meal was tea and was timed on section orders for 4pm. so if you wanted a first sitting, it was necessary to queue at about 3pm. It was at this first sitting, which consisted of one slice of bread with butter and a mug of tea, that the "rumpus" started. After an unsatisfactory dinner and a tea, several NCO's sent for the Orderly Officer. The troops in the dining hut would not commence tea nor would they let any more men into the hut. They all said they wanted to see their Orderly Officer about the tea, before they ate, or left the hut. While they were waiting for the officer, they were rattling tin plates and basins on the table, making an awful racket. The men, who were lined up outside the hut for the second sitting, were pushing the door to get inside, but those inside wouldn't let them and so it started. Someone threw a tin plate through one of the windows and others followed in quick succession. These little incidents had an effect like a lighted match on a pile of straw. The Orderly Officer didn't come, so the troops inside started to look for more bread. Tables were overturned, basins were broken and gas stoves upturned in the rush. The troops rushed into the cookhouse, throwing basins and tin plates through the windows and shouting "The War is finished now, so it's our turn to get what we want". By now it was nearly 5pm and large numbers of men who had been waiting for the second sitting hadn't had tea, so they were in a terrible mood. Several Regimental Sergeant Majors and Orderly Sergeants came to see what the trouble was, but it was too late, the troops had their backs up and there was no stopping them.

The Sergeants Messing Quarters were situated close by, which was rather a neat little hut with rustic works at the entrance. The bulk of troops, which included those who had been in the dining hut moved towards the Sergeants Mess Hut. It was quite dark now and every hut and building was lit up, including this Sergeant's hut. A Sergeant stood in the doorway on the raised step and he seemed to be arguing with the front of the crowd of troops, who were shouting and throwing tin plates etc. All of a sudden, some troops rushed for the doorway of the Mess. Several of the more daring spirits rushed inside and the Sergeants hooked it out through the back door. One of the rioters at the door of the hut asked the men outside to make way, as there were some WAAC's[78] inside. Just like true British Tommie's where women are concerned, the crowd parted in the middle, just as if it had been cleared by some gigantic knife. Then through the pathway came two members of WAAC's: who passed without any molestation or harm. After they passed, the crowd closed in again and went for the hut in force. The amount of people inside was already considerable and they were busy ransacking, taking spirits, wines etc., which was stocked

78 Women's Auxiliary Army Corps

by the Sergeants for Christmas. You can imagine the effect that stuff had on the great number of troops, drunk wasn't the name for it, singing, shouting, smashing windows and the clash of broken glass. Then suddenly, tongues of liquid flame started to lick their way up one side of the hut, those inside staggered outside into the dense mass of troops. The bulk of them drew back out of harm's way as it went up in a blazing mass. In a matter of half an hour it was gutted to the ground. By now the crowd of troops had increased to countless numbers. Close to the burning hut was the hut of the "Camp Padre". This particular chap stood in his doorway and asked what the trouble was and was told in various ways that we were not getting sufficiently fed. He then said, "Well boys. I haven't got anything for you surely you know where to get it. There are several canteens in the camp", then he pointed in the direction of one of the BEF Canteens. The troops took their own meaning of the Padre's words and pushed their way through lines of tents, several of which were knocked over and made their way to a large BEF canteen. They rushed inside, forced the assistants to leave and helped themselves to the contents. I went inside to get what I could along with the rest. Four Tommie's were standing on the counter greatly intoxicated, reaching over the shelves on which was stacked the various articles and eatables. They grabbed hold of a packet of Birds Custard Powder in each hand, turned to the pushing crowd below and said, 'Who wants this, all right nobody", well take it and share it amongst yourselves. They then threw the packets into the mass of troops and the effect was laughable, the yellow custard went all over them and made them look like canaries.

The canteen had a "Wet department" attached, with barrels of beer, whisky and wines. So the troops were getting more and more intoxicated with every passing moment. When I saw this happening, I thought I had better leave, but had an awful struggle. I took my provisions to the tent and came back to see the canteen in flames, with troops rushing out of the doors and windows. It was burnt to the ground with the glare from the Sergeant's hut and canteen lighting up the whole district. Just opposite the canteen on the other side of the road was a Church Army and Salvation Army canteen. Fortunately neither was harmed. Nearly every Tommy had something in his hands, bottles of whisky, wine and boxes of chocolates. I left the crowd to go to the Church Army Hut, a Guardsman came in and told me he had been writing a letter in the Guards Section of the camp, when suddenly the alarm went off and 150 Guardsmen in their tents fell in on parade. They were told to arm with rifles and were issued with ball cartridges, then the Officer gave the order to march. They marched about a hundred yards when word was passed through the ranks that one Guardsman had put his rifle away and hooked it out of the Guards' Section before names were taken. Whilst I was in the Church Army Hut, the crowd split into two batches, one batch had proceeded along the road to another BEF canteen in the RGA section. Naturally, when the soldiers in the RGA section saw other soldiers coming along towards camp in an uncontrolled mob, some drunk, others were carrying chocolate, cigars, cigarettes, tobacco, boots etc., we were not long in falling in with the rioters.

The RGA canteen was looted, set on fire and burnt to the ground, leaving numbers of soldiers drunk and incapable of moving. They were lying on the floor amongst the upturned forms, chairs and boxes etc., others were outside close to the wooden walls of the hut absolutely speechless. I even helped to drag men from the blazing hut. There were rumours of men being found burnt to death as they lay either in or outside the canteen. Whilst this fire was raging, a portion of the crowd proceeded to a large hut, namely the RGA Guard Room, with several soldiers who were confined for some paltry offences. There were also camp offices, clothing stores and equipment stores attached. The mob liberated the premises, set fire to the whole hut, which went up in a mass of flames, then eventually burnt to the ground. Suddenly amid the din of crackling wood and shouts from drunken soldiers was heard the clanging of the fire engine bells that came from Harfleur. The French firemen were hanging onto the sides as it approached the fire. As soon as the majority of the crowds were aware of its presence they started booing and hissing, whilst the firemen were reeling out the hosepipes and connecting the hydrants. The troops started to stone the firemen then rushed at the fire engine, smashed everything they could breaking the hose connections, cutting the hosepipes in several places and puncturing the tyres. The French Fireman couldn't stand this, so they went away and the fires burnt on. I than saw a Staff Officer in a car, which was held up by the dense mass of troops on the road. He stood on the rear seat trying to speak to the soldiers in the immediate vicinity, but to no avail, they even threw stones and lumps of earth at him. His red banded hat was knocked off, his car had the windscreen splintered so he took the hint and left.

This was now nearly midnight, with four fires burning lighting up the camp with an awesome glare. Crowds of troops were wandering aimlessly about, great numbers of them were totally drunk, some singing and shouting as if they hadn't a care in the world. Nobody in authority seemed to be making any preparations to put an end to it all, no doubt they thought it best to let the troops have their fling. It was now 12.30am, so I went to bed and lay wondering what would happen tomorrow.

The following day, which was the 10th December 1918 no reveille was sounded. At about 10am, Staff Officers motored around the camp inspecting the damage. The men were hanging around their respective tents and drill was "taboo". Section Officers were busy late in the morning trying to get a good number of men on parade, which was done after a friendly meeting with the Section Officer. He asked men who were present, for one NCO and a Private to step forward and volunteer to represent their respective sections at an enquiry, which was to be held by a General at 11am. After it had been held, there were some remarkable improvements made we had as much as we could eat at every meal. The men in credit with their pay could get as much as up to 50 Francs on payday. Greatly increased numbers of passes to Le Havre were issued to those who asked for them. I believe it was the third day after the riots that the first real parade was held just like before all the trouble.

There was a game that was routine in the camps and bases etc, called "John Brown Says". The Instructor in charge of the game used to get all his men in front of him and used to shout "John Brown says", then a pause and then "Stand on your head", then there was a scramble amongst the men to do what "John Brown says". This was carried out to make the men laugh and to take all thoughts of war and its horrors out of their minds, at least for a period," John Brown says" always had to be something silly, such as stand on one leg and hold your nose with your left hand. The Instructor would be looking for any man who hadn't carried out "John Brown's Orders". If anyone failed, he would shout "Come up, Come up" and the man would go up a difficult slope of ground. When he got beside him, he had to bend down and was given two blows across his rear with a hard cloth baton He joined the remainder of men again amid roars of laughter.

The Squad I was with had three to four hundred men, with the usual dull ground for Signallers on a high hill called the "Pimple". From the level of the camp to the top of the "Pimple", the distance was about three hundred yards. The ground became steeper, so going up alone was a hardship. We had just reached the top of the "Pimple" when a loud voice called out "John Brown says about turn", so every man immediately turned about and marched away from the path. We Signallers kept marching, taking no notice of several instructors to halt. We marched on laughing and singing, eventually reaching the main road that ran through the camp. Every man went his own way until the whole parade was somehow swallowed up. This sort of thing happened all over the camp, so there was no drill done that day. Each day following this, there was ample evidence of the drastic methods the Higher Command were putting into operation. Large numbers of men were leaving camp in full marching order for destinations unknown. It was quite evident that they meant to clear the camp regardless of where the men went.

I was sent away on the eighth day after the riots. There were about eight hundred of us who set off with a Brass Band in front. We marched by the road right to Le Havre city. As we marched through some of the main streets, we were singing all the old favourite songs and ditties. Eventually, we arrived at the railway sidings of Le Havre Station, having been halted alongside a train of the usual "Cattle Trucks". The Officer in charge and RTO were busy putting the men into each truck, they started at the engine, but trouble was in store. The problems started when our Officer, a Railway Transport Officer and Sergeant Major all stood next to the truck. In the doorway was a Corporal of the Artillery with men climbing into it two at a time. The Officer counted out aloud as they got in. On reaching number 25, the Corporal immediately stretched his arms right across the doorway and said in a loud voice "No more men for this truck there is plenty in now", everybody was struck at this display of insubordination. The Officer had commanded more men to climb aboard, but the soldiers were in a spirit of revolt and refused, which meant the whole entrainment was at a standstill. Then the Corporal responsible told the Officer, Sergeant Major and the large body of troops gathered around, his reason for taking these steps. The Corporal said that while the war was on, every soldier had to tolerate a great deal of inconvenience whilst travelling in these trucks, sometimes travelling with forty men in each compartment. He said the troops did this without complaining, knowing full well that every inch of room was needed for the conveyance of the materials of war such as guns, ammunition systems etc. He said now the war was over, he for one was determined these conditions were not going to be repeated if he could help it. After this speech, the men who were gathered around cheered him again and again. Other Sergeants and Corporals from the camp took matters into their own hands and supervised the loading and wouldn't allow more than 25 into any truck. The Officers and Sergeant Major in charge were helpless. Fortunately the train was loaded up, leaving about a third of the troops left on the platform.

Each truck was loaded with 25 men instead of 40, resulting in these men not being able to board. The Officers tried again and again to get the men on the platform into the trucks, but troops inside wouldn't allow it and those outside never tried. At last the train moved off with hearty cheers from those in the trucks and the men left behind.

We travelled on at a slow speed, eventually reaching St. Pol where we detrained. From St. POL, we boarded a light railway conveyance, then arrived at a large Infantry Musketry Training Camp. Having arrived we were on the parade ground waiting to see what they were going to do with us. The Camp Commander came and told us he didn't know anything about us coming, but he would do his best. If we had patience, he would get the cooks to prepare a meal for us and on the next day he would see what he could do to get us some pay. After this kind talk, we dispersed into the huts, then after an hour or so, we had a good feed of nourishing stew and bread.

On the next day, we had our breakfast of bacon, bread and tea and at about 11am we were paraded, when each man received 5 Francs with the excuse that it was the best they could do at short notice. Then on the third day, we marched out again and were entrained at St. POL. eventually reaching Lille. At Lille we were split up into batches and sent different ways to various units. I along with a dozen others was sent to the 203rd Brigade Ammunition Column which was camped on a hillside in an awful state, mud all over.

The day I arrived they were making preparations to move. This was done on the following day during a continuous downpour when I got soaked to the skin. We marched the next day with wet clothes, then eventually camped at about 8pm outside a broken down village. As is usually the case with new reinforcements to a unit, I was put in charge of the Picquet and Guard for the night. I visited my Sentries several times, always in heavy rain, that didn't stop until morning. At 6am the Guard and Picquet were dismissed and ordered into the stables, but I didn't go because I wasn't feeling very well I went to my billet in a room of a broken down house, which had a wire bed, took my wet clothes off and lay down. I had no sooner laid my head down, than stabbing pains started to shoot across my forehead, back and legs and I was sweating profusely. The billet Orderly asked me if I was ill, then went to get me two extra blankets and a large pot of tea, which I was very thankful for. At 8pm the men were dismissed from the stables for breakfast and one chap brought some bacon and dipped bread, but I couldn't eat it. The bugles went for parade again at 9am, but I lay still. At about 9.15am the subsection Sergeant came around the billets looking for "sulkers'" from parade. He saw me lying in bed and immediately ordered me to get on parade. I told him that I was ill and wanted to see the Doctor. He said that I was an "old soldier" and again ordered me out of bed, saying that if I didn't get up within 15 minutes he would have me up in front of the C.O. "All right Sergeant" I said, "I'll get up, but not to go on parade. I'm going to see the Doctor and I'll report to you when I'm there". I got out of bed, but could hardly stand, I was that weak. I struggled down the village to see the Doctor. As soon as he looked into my face, he jumped off his chair and shouted for an Orderly, "Put this chap on a stretcher immediately" he said. The Doctor took my temperature, which was 102' and said I should never have left my billet I told him my Sergeant had ordered me on parade, in spite of me being ill and I had only managed to get to him from sheer desperation. The Doctor took the Sergeant's name and said that he would have him attended to. Soon after this, I was put into an ambulance and taken to Hospital, which was a large tent with about 50 beds. I was given pills, with nothing to eat or drink, but milk food and was there for 6 days.

After this period I was put on a stretcher again and taken to some Red Cross cars. We eventually arrived at a railway siding and were put into an ambulance train. When it was fully loaded, it travelled very slowly, so about 30 hours later we reached Le Havre. When it stopped, I could see out of the window the masts and funnels of ships, which were close to us. Immediately my hopes were raised of getting to Blighty. We were all taken from the train and laid on the platform.

During our stay numbers of women and church people came and spoke to us. They gave us fags and chocolates etc., the whole platform was clad with stretchers and I could see batches of RAMC men carrying them from the far end of the platform. Eventually, I was picked up, carried out of the station and contrary to my hopes, I was placed into a Red Cross Car along with the other three. It was quite dark and as we travelled through the streets, I caught fleeting glimpses of street lamps and lighted shop windows. We stopped outside a large building, I was carried in, given a bath and put to bed, I learned later it was called "The Casino" and run on strict business lines. Patients were not allowed to talk loudly and had to conform strictly to rules and regulations. It was while I was a patient in this Hospital that I was very ill for a period of 8 days and had no bowel motion until they were forced to give me an injection.

After a stay of one month, I was sent to a large Convalescent Camp, which was on high ground on the outskirts of Le Havre. I was one of a batch of two hundred or so, who were sent from the Hospital. When we arrived we were paraded in the largest hut and told to make ourselves comfortable until the Camp Major came. After giving us a hearty welcome, he told us we were to get strong and if we didn't, it wouldn't be his fault, then we all started to laugh. The Officer told us that we would be at the camp for a fortnight, then at the end of that time, each man would have to be examined, to see if he was well enough to go back to his usual duties. He also said each man would be asked on his honour as a British Soldier, if he would like another week, or if he felt he was strong enough to go back to duty. If he said another week would do him a great deal of good, he would be permitted to stay. He then told us his idea of running a Convalescent Camp was to see for himself that each man had the best possible chance of getting well before going away and said he had never up to that time, had any complaints from any man about his treatment, or having been sent away from the Camp before he was strong enough. After this speech, the men cheered themselves hoarse I have never heard an

Officer speak with so much feeling, it was very unusual to hear such expressions from a man with a great deal of responsibility.

The fortnight passed over quickly and we never worked, as all duties were done by permanent staff. Every night we could get a pass from 5pm until 10pm to go into Le Havre, needless to say the Camp was empty every night. Then the medical examination day arrived to determine who had to leave the Camp for duty.

All of us were paraded and marched into a hut in single file we passed on through the hut to the far end where the Commandant and the Doctor were standing. As each man came up to them he was taken to one side and asked by the Doctor if he felt strong and well? Did he think he would benefit by another week, and how long had he been in the firing line? If a man said that he would like another week and he had been in France more than 18 months he was always allowed to stay. A great number of men said that they were quite strong and well. I said I would like another week, which I was given. At the end of three weeks, I left the camp with very pleasant memories of fun, games, sports, music, good food and above all, a reverent respect for an Officer, a man who put his men's health and well-being first.

Chapter 12

L'envoi

From this camp I was sent to Harfleur once again but it was in a different condition to my previous stay. I was only there for three days this time and was sent off with a large batch of reinforcements. After some wearisome travelling in the trucks, we reached Lille. We spent a day or two hanging about while several of us were distributed to various units. I was included in a dozen reinforcements for a unit in Belgium. We boarded a motor lorry and set off, after about two hours we dismounted at Tournai. We then marched to the village of Vaulx, eventually being joined with the 107 Brigade RFA where another Bombardier and I were placed with the First Battery.

We were billeted with a young Belgian couple who were very nice to us. We used to help the young man grind his corn meal into flour and as a reward we were given a large cake, we had some very happy nights together. One Sunday night, my friend and I were sitting around the stove reading, when there was a knock at the door. The wife answered and there was a great babble of voices of men, then into the kitchen trooped about fifteen young Belgian men. Each of them had some unusual instruments ranging from cornets to big trumpets.

They settled themselves down in a circle around the kitchen and started to play with the Bandmaster in the middle of the floor. You couldn't hear yourself speak, but it was an enjoyable evening.

I then received a letter from my eldest brother who had been in the Anti-Aircraft Section in France and Belgium since late September 1915. The last time I saw him was at the early end of 1915 in York Station, he was returning from his leave at Newcastle and I was stationed at York. I had obtained leave to go to York Station to see him for a few minutes while his train was there. His letter told me that he was at Lille, but he didn't know where I was. I knew that Lille was about 30 or 40 kilometres away from me and I was determined to see him by hook or by crook. I saw my Sergeant Major and explained everything to him. He was very sympathetic and promised he would try and get me a weekend off, I received it and set off at 7.30am on the Saturday.

I reached Tournai at about 9am, then stood at the beginning of the main road to Lille. My intention was to jump motor lorries to get me there quicker, but when I saw our own lorries going to Lille, I was very surprised to see every one of them full of mostly women civilians. I tried several times, but it was useless, so rather than waste any more time, I decided to walk the whole way. I knew it was a long job but I was very cheerful about it. I had my weekend rations in a sandbag over my shoulder and off I went, Dick Whittington style, along the road to Lille. I kept on the roadway on the off chance that I would get picked up by some lorry or other conveyance. I continued until I reached the outskirts of Tournai, with the broad main road stretching like a huge serpent before me for miles. I heard a car behind me and when I looked around. I saw a Red Cross Ambulance coming towards me. I stood in the centre of the road, held up my hand and was very pleased when the driver pulled up. I asked for a lift into Lille and was told to get inside. When I peered inside the car I noticed it was full of Belgian civilians with two of our Royal Engineer Corps. I managed to get inside then sat on the piece of boarding at the rear, which was very uncomfortable. During the journey I got into conversation with the two Engineers, who were also going to Lille, but had some trouble getting a lift. They told me they had come from Brussels that morning and every lorry and car was chock-a-block with Belgians.

On nearing Lille, the driver shouted to us three Tommie's that we should all have to get out when we reached the outskirts, as he didn't want to be seen bringing civilians in a Red Cross car. The Engineers and I decided we might as well try to get a few Francs out of the Belgian civilians to compensate the driver for his trouble and kindness. I took off my hat and put two Francs into it, then held it in front of the two Engineers, who did likewise and tried to explain to them what it was for. After we had passed the hat around we had 25 Francs, which we gave to the Driver. He thanked us very much and said he wouldn't take the lot, gave us 5 Francs each and kept 10 Francs for himself. After all the civilians had left, I was very pleased to leave as I was very sore from sitting in a cramped state.

I made my way to Lille and was very impressed with the city. Having enquired about the place where my brother was I found out I would have to walk to the other side of Lille. I eventually saw a large building in front of me, which was my brother's billet, so I went and asked for his Section. I went upstairs into a large room where there were several Artillerymen sitting on their beds and looked around to see if my brother was there, suddenly, I saw him sitting on his bed. Nearly everyone in the room was looking at me, but not him; no doubt they saw I was a stranger. I walked slowly towards him with a smile on my face, then just as I was about 6 yards away, he raised his head and looked into my face. His face lit up, then a smile spread across it as he recognised me. We shook hands with a tight grip and didn't speak for a few seconds. We then sat down on his bed and began to talk. He introduced me to his pals and when he told them where I came from, they were amazed at my pluck. I had arrived at a very opportune time (dinner time) and being as I was unexpected, my brother had to hunt for some dinner for me.

We both got ready then went off to Lille at about 5pm. We made a tour of the Estaminets, though not as we would have both liked, as money was very scarce between us. We had a decent time considering our resources and were very contented when we tucked into his bed that night. We got up early the next morning (Sunday), had a good breakfast and went for another stroll around, getting back for dinner. After dinner, we sat talking about home and war experiences and towards teatime, I prepared to go back to Tournai.

After tea we made our way to the other side of Lille to get onto the main road to Tournai. My brother said we would make for the station in the hope that I would get a ration train going to Tournai. He told me he often did guard duty on these trains between Lille and Tournai and that the trains ran pretty frequently. We reached the station and saw the NCO in charge, who my brother knew, but our hopes were blighted. He said he couldn't give us any definite time as to when the next train would come through as the line had been disorganised lately. He said there might he one in 5 minutes; then again it might be 5 hours. We waited for about half an hour, then I started to get anxious, I knew the only sure way was walking. After consulting, my brother and I decided to get going, so off we went onto the main road to Tournai. We talked about different things until we were in the suburbs of Lille. I repeatedly told him to go back as I was all right and would get back to my unit by Monday morning. We passed the outskirts of Lille and walked along the broad stone paved road without a house in sight. Before us stretched the bleak surrounding countryside, the gaunt trees standing on the roadside like Sentinels, with the sky turning black as dusk was setting in. I stopped suddenly and held out my hand to my brother, shook it and told him not to come any further and said "So long". I turned away to hide a tear and set off at a good pace with my face towards Tournai and the gathering darkness I kept looking around periodically to see my brother with his hand up, eventually becoming a faint dim figure in the far distance, which was soon swallowed up by the quick gathering night.

On losing sight of him, an awful sense of loneliness came over me. There I was walking along the main road through the open country without habitation and in absolute darkness I carried on at the same fast pace with my ears alert for any noise of motor traffic that might come along. I never heard a sound, only those quiet night noises that one cannot understand.

I was a good way into my journey and feeling so tired, I felt I could lie down where I was and go to sleep. The loneliness was awful and I kept turning my head around again and again, expecting to see someone behind me. Then I saw shapes ahead and when I got further, I saw it was a village with every place in darkness, except for one house. I approached to find thin streaks of light shining through cracks in the window shutters; I knew it was an Estaminet. I knocked at the door but got no answer, I knocked again and heard the rattling of chains and drawing of bolts. The door opened about 6 inches and I saw the face of an old man. Not being able to speak Belgian, I did the best I could and said "Cafe Messeur, resti ici?" He opened the door and I went into the room, sat down and pulled out the remainder of my rations. I put them on the table and asked the old man for coffee, which he brought in a very small basin. I pushed it away and mimed with my hands that I wanted a big one. He looked surprised, but brought it. It was a drink that I wanted as much as anything. He charged me half a Franc, which surprised me, as it was cheap considering I had a pint and a half of coffee in the large basin. I had some cheese and bread from my rations, a rest and smoke then got up to leave. I had a good half a loaf, a tin of Fray Bentos Corned Beef from my rations so I gave them to the old man who bowed and thanked me continuously as I passed into the darkness.

The darkness seemed to be denser than ever, so I had to go slowly as my eyes weren't tuned to the blackness. I was in the countryside and had been walking for about 15 minutes when I heard the rumble of wheels in the distance, so I stopped hoping it was a lorry going to Tournai. The rumble of the wheels drew nearer. I knew it was going my way at last, so I stood in the middle of the road waving my arms over my head. I saw the lorries lamps were oil, therefore they didn't cast much light, so I had to get into the roadside to avoid being knocked down. As it passed by, I made a run to take hold of the back; my heart nearly sank, as it was one of the high back types, so found it hard to grasp the back board. I was forced to keep running behind or let go, but this was the last thing I wanted to do. I had my overcoat on which made it harder for me. At last I made a superhuman effort to climb up into the back of the lorry. I succeeded in getting in so far with the edge of the back board across my chest, with my head and half of my chest almost in the lorry, with the lower part of my body dangling outside. I lay clinging on in sheer desperation being bumped and tossed about by the rolling of the lorry over uneven parts of the roadway. I couldn't seem to find the strength to make an effort to pull myself up, but eventually I made a special effort and rolled inside. The lorry was three parts full of coal dust and I landed right in it. The driver said "Who's there?" No doubt he and his mate heard me scuffling about. I told them where I had been and where I was going and they told me that they would put me off in Tournai. I was very pleased and dosed off into a sort of sleep I eventually reached Tournai about 12.30am on the Monday morning.

I then made my way back to Vaulx, the village where I was billeted as it was only about 7 or 8 kilometres away. It didn't take me long and I was back for roll call on first parade at 6.30am. I didn't go to the stables like the rest of the Battery, "Oh No". I dodged the column and went back to my billet to sleep until breakfast time.

Time in this small village hung heavily upon us. There were just the usual stable duties and guard and piquet posts to attend to. Our horses were being gradually taken away from us to be sold. Men were continually leaving us to go home for good.

Our Officers arranged a concert party, there were several good artists left amongst the Battery and after a good deal of rehearsing, we had a passable show. A large hall was used for the theatre, with a stage rigged up, but the drawback was three large holes in the walls near the stage, so these had to be blocked up. The Sergeant Major was discussing ways of doing this one day, when he thought he hit upon the proper solution. I was acting Battery Orderly at the time, so the Sergeant Major gave me orders to get the six men out of "clink", who were in for various minor offences. He told me to take them to the stables, get a wagon and four horses, then go to some ruins nearby, to fill the wagon with bricks from the broken down walls of the houses. I had to then take them to the Hall or 'Theatre' and get the six men to put the bricks into the holes in the wall. I thought it was a joke, as we had no proper tools, mortar or staging, which was all necessary to do the job. But orders in the Army had to be carried out. So I set about the task. The first official performance of our concert party was notified for a fortnights time; therefore I was given this time to block the holes up. Our first puzzle was how to get mortar or plaster to set the bricks. This was done with ordinary earth mixed with water into a slimy mess, and then the bricks were cleaned of the old plaster, which took a great deal of time. The staging had to be put up, with beer barrels and planks of wood. After three days I and six men got started on the task of filling the holes and we got along very well, considering our inexperience. By the time the first performance came round we only had two of the holes finished, the other was too high up the wall for us to reach. When the Sergeant Major came to inspect our work, he remarked that it didn't look neat, but it would stop the draught. Then came the evening of the first performance, all the Battery and civilians from the village were invited, what a crowd.

The hall was packed with Belgian men, women and children all jabbering together. Then on came the first turn, it was a humorous sketch of husband and wife in their bedroom preparing for bed, arguing about the war. German Zeppelins were supposed to be heard coming overhead, so the wife was frantic with fear. During the sketch the civilians were laughing and clapping hands, just as if they understood every word. The curtain fell at the conclusion of the sketch and the people were shuffling in their seats, when there was such a crash at the side of the Hall. My first thoughts were "Oh Christ, our wall" and I was right. There sure enough, was our fortnight's work lying on the floor inside the hall, with the moon shining through the holes. I couldn't get off my seat for laughing then the Sergeant Major came over. He looked up at the holes, rubbed his chin with his hand, then turned and looked at me. He must have been tickled by the grin on my face because he started to laugh and walked up towards the stage. The performance carried on with the wind blowing through the hall.

Then one day while doing a little clerical work in the Battery's office, I saw an order for one man to go home to the Ripon area. Knowing that I was the only North Country man from this area, I was overjoyed at the prospect of getting home. I was eventually warned to pack up and prepare to go to Boulogne with the Demobilisation Team that left Tournai on a certain date. I left my billet with the good wishes of our Belgian friend and wife.

When I arrived in Tournai I was put into a camp, all going home. We stayed here for two days until all the men going home from the surrounding district had arrived. Then on the third morning we marched through the streets of Tournai with a Military Brass Band leading us. We were all very happy as we marched along singing all the Army songs. We reached the station and were put into the usual covered in trucks but these were different inside to the ones I had known. There was a form to sit on around the side and a large iron stove in the centre. After we were entrained, Officers came along and shouted at each truck for two men to go to the head of the train to obtain rations of coal and candles for their respective trucks. This was very unusual, as we generally had to provide our own candles and pinch the coal from the engine. We were very thankful for them because during the night on our journey, we would have been very cold without the fire.

We halted about 2am in the middle of some awful desolate countryside. The moon was casting its rays over snow clad ground. It was a lovely scene, but it also made our flesh creep. Alongside the roadway were half a dozen tents with several large fires and when we arrived, we found tea and bully sandwiches, it was a welcome surprise which everyone appreciated We were soon on our way again and at about 8am we were nearing Boulogne, but it didn't take us long to get out and on our way to camp. The camp was one which nearly every one of us was familiar with, namely St. Martin's Camp[79] on the hill. When we did eventually get into the camp, we found it was a different part to the one we thought. The St. Martin's Camp proper that all troops going and coming from England always stayed at, was on the opposite side of the hill to our camp. We were told this camp was a clearing centre for troops going home.

The first day here, we were put into huts and given a good hot meal at dinnertime, tea was also very good. On the second day, every man was paraded in a large open space, then marched to a series of large huts, which were built together forming one large wooden block. Into this block of buildings we went in batches of 100 or so. When inside we found forms and wooden erections similar to an ordinary clothes-horse, which is common in working class houses in England. On each of these clotheshorses, there were about forty metal clothes pegs, twenty on each side. Each man had to choose a peg to hang his clothes on. On each peg were two loops of string and tied to each string was a piece of wood with a number exactly the same. Tied to the other were all different numbers As each man had fully undressed and stood in the garb of "Adam", he was told to hang a piece of wood on the peg his clothes were on and hang the other piece of wood around his neck. There was a number on the clothes and the same number around the neck of the owner. After this operation was completed,

79 St Martin's Camp was a large camp on the site of a Napoleonic Camp and was used throughout the war as a concentration area for individual reinforcements, training and at the end of the war for repatriation. Like Harfleur these were not easy camps to run and discontent was frequently rife. This is often the case when soldiers are not in formed units where the influence of discipline and loyalty to Regiment or Corps are strong.

there were about a hundred men of all ages, shapes and sizes standing about with no clothes on, we were all ushered into another part of the building where there was a concrete floor, with several sinks in it. Overhead were rows of iron pipes about three inches in diameter. In these pipes were holes at intervals and through these hot water was flowing pretty fast. On the concrete floor were large pieces of carbolic soap and long handled brushes. Needless to say, each man knew what was wanted of him. Soon the floor was a mass of soapy water with men standing there, rubbing and scrubbing themselves as if they had never washed before. What a good picture it would have made. Soon everyone was washed, cleaned and dried and we were taken from room to room where stoves were used for heating. The air was nice and warm with every man sitting or walking about. Batches of six were taken away into a small recess, which was curtained off. In there were two doctors and about six RAMC Orderlies. As each man got into the recess, he had to see the Doctor. He would hold up each of the soldiers' arms at full length, then put a large magnifying glass close to the hair under his arms. This was repeated on every part of the soldier's body where hair grew. The soldier before me had all his hair on the abdomen lathered with soap and hot water later having it shaved off. I passed out as clean, and then was ushered into a large room where all men who had previously passed through were sitting naked, except for the piece of wood with a number on around their neck. Jokes were cheap and not too clean, but as everyone was male, it didn't matter much. At different intervals, Orderlies at the camp would wheel several clotheshorses in. Then there was a rush of naked men to see if the clothes had the same number on their neck. It went on until every man was standing outside fully dressed. I learned that while each man had been passing through, his clothes had been taken away and fumigated, or cleaned and disinfected to kill all vermin. The men who had their hair shaved, had lice eggs. These were precautions taken to ensure that each man returned home to England absolutely clean and free from vermin.

The following day, we were all taken across the valley to St. Martin's Camp proper, then stayed there until a ship could be provided to take us to England. After breakfast we could get to Boulogne but only up until 9.30am, which was a privilege that was used very much. On the second morning in the camp, we were all lined up at the dining hut door waiting to go in for breakfast. Snow was thick upon the ground with an icy wind blowing. Every man was stamping about cursing the cooks for keeping us waiting. Each man passed the cook who filled his mess tin with tea, onto the second who gave him two rounds of bread, then the third for a large tin of Tyne Brand Herrings, then into the hut to have his breakfast. After every man had left the dining hut, it was just like a fish market, tins of herring and bread lying about all over. No one could find an appetite on such a cold morning to eat tinned herring. The next morning the troops hoped we would have bacon and dip, but no we went to the first cook for tea, second cook for bread and third cook was standing in front of a large galvanised iron bath with a large wooden spoon. He would call out "Want any herring?" with a devilish smile, then plunges his spoon into the mashed up fish. Every soldier pinched his nose and hurried into the dining hut to eat his dry bread and tea, such is Army life.

At 10am we were all called on parade with full equipment, and then we marched to the docks with civilians waving their hands and throwing kisses. After about half an hour we were taken on board the 'Royal Scot' and left Boulogne at 1pm on 14th February 1919. We arrived at Tilbury at 8pm. As it was dark we weren't allowed to disembark until the next day. So we made ourselves as comfortable as possible for that night. Early the next morning we were awoke and soon we were taken of the ship in small tugboats. After landing once more on English soil we were as pleased as anyone could wish to be. We were taken to a large shed where we were given a parcel of eatables and pot of cocoa. We then entrained at Tilbury Station and at 10am prompt on 15th February, we started our journey to Ripon.

After an uneventful journey, we arrived at Ripon Dispersal Camp at 1 30am on 16th February, where we were given hot meals and told that reveille would be at 8am. We had good beds and didn't need rocking to sleep. The next day after breakfast, we entered some huts to hand in various articles of equipment. We eventually stood ready to leave with our tin hat, overcoat, sandbag and our various personal belongings. Then off to Ripon station for the last stage of the journey.

When I arrived, I decided to send a telegram to my wife saying I was coming home and obtained a wire form, filled it in and when I looked for the money to pay, I found to my horror that I only had French notes. I tried to get change from the other troops, but every one was in the same predicament, so I couldn't send it. We left Ripon amid cheers and farewells from various civilians who settled down in our carriage, full of nervous excitement at the prospect of being home in an hour or two. At 1pm the train drew to a stop at Newcastle Central Station, then I marched across the platform with a brisk step. I anxiously scanned the people standing about to see if my wife was there, or any other relatives, but was disappointed. I left the station to make my way, with my tin hat and sandbag over my shoulder. I was about half way home when I observed my wife wheeling the pram with one of my kiddies in, on the same footpath, coming towards me. I stood in their path and waited until she came up to me, she halted to get past a man who was standing in the way of the pram. When she looked into my face, recognition was immediate; I hugged and kissed her and the kiddie, disregarding the looks and smiles of passersby. Oh, the joy of this simple street meeting of wife and myself. We made our way home, home that I could call home once again forever.

So ended my four years in the British Army.

FINIS

Appendix 1

Ranks of Royal Artillery

<u>Commissioned Ranks</u>

Lieutenant Colonel	Command of Artillery Brigade
Major	Command of Battery
Captain	Command of Section of two guns or Gun Position Officer or Observation Officer
Lieutenant	
2nd Lieutenant	

<u>Warrant and Non Commissioned Ranks</u>

Warrant Officer 1	Regimental Sergeant Major
Warrant Officer 2	Battery Sergeant Major
Staff Sergeant	Battery Quartermaster Sergeant
Sergeant	Gun i/c or No 1
Bombardier	
Lance Bombardier	
Driver	Drove the horses of the team, 3 drivers per gun
Gunner	Gun numbers and members of the riding detachment

Appendix 2

The 18 Pound Quick Fire Gun

The 18 pdr was introduced in 1904, and was the backbone of British field artillery during and after the First World War. The original design was typical of the era, with a pole trail, shield, wooden wheels, etc - and more than 10,000 were made. Kitchener in October 1914 ordered an additional 3000 18 pdrs to support the increase of the Army. In 1916, an improved design was begun, but it was not until 1918 that this reached production as the Mk IV on Mark III Carriage.

This was a considerable improvement as it used a box trail allowing better elevation, an Asbury breech mechanism, and a hydro pneumatic recoil system. It became the standard post-war equipment, and in subsequent years was further improved by a split-trail carriage and pneumatic tyres. The hunt for a replacement (ultimately the 25pdr) began in the 1920s, and when the 25pdr Mk I was introduced, it absorbed a number of 18 pdr guns which were converted by simply changing the barrels.

Since the 25pdr was slow coming into full production, the 18 pdr remained in service for much of the war. Many marks lingered until 1944 in use as training weapons or dispersed around the country as anti-invasion weapons. It was the primary armament of several field regiments after their return from the Battle of France. Numbers remained in service in various overseas stations and during the early part of the Burma campaign. Marks ranged from Mk I (the original pattern wire wound screw breech 1904 model) to Mk V (a long list of improvements including new trail, tyres, and 37.5 degree elevation).

Data: 18pdr Gun Mk IV on Carriage Mk 5P

Weight Of Gun And Breech Mechanism	952 Lbs
Total Length	96.96 Inches
Length Of Bore	92.735 Inches
Rifling	18 Grooves, uniform Right Hand Twist 1/30
Breech Mechanism	Asbury Interrupted Screw, Percussion Fired
Elevation	-5 Degrees To 37.5 Degrees
Traverse	25 Degrees Left Or Right
Recoil System	Hydro Pneumatic 26-48 Inches Dependent On Charge
Weight In Action	3,507 Lbs

Cartridge and Projectile Performance:
(Firing The Standard 18 Lb shell)

Muzzle Velocity	1,625 ft/sec
Maximum Range	11,100 Yards

Ranges
Ranges differ according to circumstances. Normally 6,500 yards was the planning range with an added 1,000 yards if the gun was dug in.

Ammunition

In the early days of the war only shrapnel rounds were available. The shrapnel round could be adjusted to burst in the air so although effective against infantry and cavalry it was not much use against trenches. High Explosive was not introduced for the 18 pdr until 1915 although the howitzers and the heavy artillery did have HE from the start.

It is well known that by 1916 there was a severe limitation on the production of shells. Each gun potentially had 1000 rounds available. These were distributed as follows:

Limber	24
Battery Wagons	152
Brigade Ammunition Column	76
Divisional Ammunition Column	126
Base Depots	622

By the end of the war the ammunition available was HE Shell Mk 46 - Filled with TNT or Amatol, complete round weighed 23.5 Lbs and was 23.379 inches long. 1 Lb 7 Ounce propelling charge in an 11.6 inch brass cartridge. A streamlined shell (Mk 13 C) was available as were reduced charge training rounds (Mk 14), Smoke (WP filling) and Shrapnel (Mk 17) with contained 375 lead balls and had a reduced range of 9,400 yards. Finally there was also Cartridge, QF, 18pdr AP Shot Mk 3T - solid shot with tracer.

POSTSCRIPT

George returned home from the war to Newcastle to his wife and children, son, George who was born on 28th November 1914, and Mildred born on 1st November1916. He resumed his employment for W.H Smith & Sons with whom he remained employed for over 50 years. Life was difficult with many illnesses afflicting his young family. George wrote a record of occurrences of family life which makes quite depressing reading. Health and money seeming to be the family's main struggles. His diary entries are summarised below:

George and Mildred had two more daughters, Edna born on 23rd May 1918, and Lena born on 30th July 1920. In May 1922 they sadly lost their eldest daughter Mildred, (named after her mother) aged just 5, after a year of illnesses that began with Scarlet Fever. Mildred was laid to rest in Elswick Cemetery on Thursday June 1st 1922. The following March (27.03.1923) Mildred (sometimes referred to as Millie) gave birth to her fifth child a healthy boy named Angus Elder weighing 8lbs 4ozs. However Angus didn't survive his first year, he died aged 11 months on the 14th February 1924. George wrote, *"Our little baby boy Angus aged 11 months died from Pneumonia on Friday 14th at 3am after being ill since 8pm the previous evening. It was a sudden blow to us loving him as we did. He was buried on the following Monday 14th at 2pm in Elswick Cemetery with plenty of flowers and only about 20 yards away from our daughter Millie.*

George in his grief decided to buy a Retriever puppy called Nell to boost the morale of his family. However his next year was a turbulent one with all children falling ill and niggling arguments between himself and Millie whilst they were trying to come to terms with their grief. Despite their differences Millie fell pregnant with her 6th child,

George wrote on March 20th 1925: *"Millie is very heavy afoot in great pain, expecting any day."*

Baby Mabel was born on 3rd April 1925. Named after George's sister Mabel.

Smallpox was a huge killer in the 19th century and the UK introduced a mandatory vaccination campaign in 1904. In July 1925 all of the Elder children were vaccinated at home by Dr Newton, the local doctor for the Newcastle area.

1925 saw George enter his 33rd year. Money was in short supply and George made the decision to sell the family dog Nell for 10 shillings. However in February 1926, after returning to the home many times, George was forced to buy the dog back, and wrote: "*The man I sold Nell to, brings her back to say that he cannot keep her as she won't eat and is fretting. Previously, since selling her she had come back home from Dunston about 4 times and been taken away again. So considering the dog's feelings and with the persuasion of the wife and kiddies, I buy her back again and she is very content to be back at her own fireside once again.*"

The family struggle further financial difficulties during 1926 and were affected by the miners' strikes that took place during the first half of the year. Due to lack of work George applied to the RFA records office at Woolwich to enlist onto Section D Reserve Force, however he was turned down, as they were fully manned.

During 1926 George wrote consistently about Baby Mabel being poorly, and the various visits to the doctor who suggested that Mabel was not thriving. He wrote during November 1926 about the family's progress;*"Lena is getting on pretty well, though still keeping thin, rather backward in her schooling though pretty quick at home. Edna is more of a "madam" type, having rather a craze for stage work with someone to look at her and praise her. Very nervous of pain of any description, especially having a tooth drawn. George is still going on with his band etc., getting quite a good player. Goes to music practices every week at Peoples Hall, Rye Hill with his Uncle Dick. He is very good in his schooling, passing every exam and being complimented by the Teacher. He is growing into a big broad shouldered young man and at his 12th birthday, November 28th is in the best of health with the exception of chilblains in each foot. Mildred is still "nattery" though she has every excuse as things are going very bad with us financially. Rather a struggle to make ends meet. Myself, well, still jogging along best I can. Have a touch of rheumatic pains in my legs, effects of service in France during the Great War 1914-1918."*

Sadly on November 29th 1926 George had to have Nell the family dog put down as finances were too strained, and he could no longer afford to feed her. Millie also sadly suffered a miscarriage on December 5th 1926, she was 4 months pregnant, and the baby was a boy. George was very disappointed as he would have loved another son. Mille recovered well in time for Christmas.

Life didn't get much easier in 1927, George suffered with rheumatism in his legs, Millie with various ailments, including pleurisy, Lena had a tonsillectomy, Georgie required glasses which was an added expense for the family, yet more prominently George wrote of Mabel's continuing poor health.

September 5th 1927 marked the 21st Anniversary of George starting work at WH Smith. He wrote: "*This day is the 21st Anniversary of my starting work at WH Smith. I started work at that firm at the age of 14 years and 3 months. This day September 5th 1927 completes a service at the firm of exactly 21 years.*"

1928 is a mixed year for the Elder family. It began with financial hardship and illnesses for the children, however by August, George has scratched together enough money to take the family on holiday, he booked a bungalow for a week in Frenchman's Bay, and the family returned feeling refreshed. However by December, Mabel was diagnosed with Tuberculosis of the spine. After much deliberation Mabel was admitted to the Wingrove Hospital on December 22nd where her treatment commenced. Visiting days were Wednesdays and Saturdays.

George's diary entries for the first half of 1929 consist of his hospital visits to Mabel. She was fitted with a frame in order to straighten her spine in the January. In June she developed an abscess on the spine, however George and Mildred refused to give consent for an operation. Also in June, Georgie began working for book sellers called Robinsons on Nelson Street. His starting wage was 10 shillings a week.

In July of 1929 George and Mildred had a rare and exciting day out to London. George wrote: *"Millie and myself go to London to Lord Hambledon's Garden Party at Henley On Thames. Our train fare was paid by Lord Hambledon. Millie and I left Newcastle on Friday at 1.15am on 26th July. Had all that day in London sightseeing. Millie was nearly done up at night time through walking around, seeing all the principal sites during her walks, she wasn't sorry. The Garden Party on Saturday was splendid, we had a lovely time. We arrived back in Newcastle on Sunday 28th at 6.30am, pretty well fagged out with travelling, but well satisfied with ourselves. Georgie is well established in the Gloops Band, they had a concert party in the new City Hall, which was a great success. Uncle Dick was very pleased with his band's performance. He is still working at Robinson's shop and pretty well satisfied. Mabel is going on as well as can be expected, but she is beginning to feel it when we leave her each rainy day."*

The latter part of the year saw Lena suffer with Rheumatic fever and then Saint Vitus Dance, which is also known as Choreia, this is an abnormal involuntary movement disorder, generally affecting the hands and feet. The patient appears to be dancing, hence the name. Mildred suffered with an ulcerated leg and was bed bound for over 2 weeks.

1930 began on a better note, Mabel had a new frame fitted, and started to stand and walk a few steps. Lena recovered and returns to school having cost the family two pounds and ten shillings in doctors' fees. Georgie joined a dance band in Heaton; however his father was concerned about the continuous late nights for his son, and comments on him coming home past 11pm every night.

In May 1930, the family moved away from Sycamore Street into a 2 room house at 9 Bowman Terrace. George describes it as healthier all round for the family. July came and the family managed a holiday to a place called Shores Wood, near Norsham, just outside Berwick upon Tweed.

April 1931 finally see's Mabel discharged from the Wingrove Hospital. Her total length of stay was 2 years and 4 months. Mabel was in hospital from Christmas 1928, aged 3 and a half to April 1931, aged 6 years.

August 1931 and the Elder family moved home once more. The new residence is in St. Cuthbert's Terrace, and George again suggests how this is a much healthier environment for his growing family. Mabel attended an open air school called Pendower School which was built in 1925 in an attempt to combat the high rate of serious illness among schoolchildren.

George didn't write again until 1933 when the family moved home once more. Their new address was 62 Tullock Street, Newcastle. George wrote of the move: "*Removed to 62 Tullock Street, Newcastle in March, 5 roomed house and scullery – 15/- per week, a very heavy rent, but we manage somehow. George is still at Dex Garage, but Edna still has a task to get employment. She is doing some sort of housework three days per week for 3/- to 4/-, not much but it helps a little. Lena has been off school now for a few weeks, having been to the Infirmary about her heart trouble which is thought to be caused by rheumatism. She is picking up wonderfully now. Mabel is growing into a very fine girl. Tall and plump and very quick at picking things up. She is learning wonderfully at school, reading and writing and sums etc. She still attends Pendower School and it has done her an immensity of good.*"

Millie turned 40 this year and George lost his father in the July after a series of operations on his enlarged bladder.

1934, George celebrated his 42nd birthday and updates his diary as below:

"*Forty two years old on 16th instant and feel it. Millie is a little ratty* *now and then, but nothing serious. George is now a fine young man, getting on fine with his music. He is one of a Dance Band that has been formed and I believe that their first dance is on the 13th August 1934 after being postponed a few times. He is still working at Dex Garage, but it's only a few hours which is not to his or our liking. Edna is at Mrs. Orr's place as in Maple Street as a Day Girl. She doesn't seem to do much work because she is home every afternoon. Rather a wayward girl is Edna; in fact I am rather worrying about her. She seems so obstinate at times and seems bent on having her own way. This mood of hers had brought her a number of thrashings, even at her age 16½ years. I sincerely hope that as years come upon her she will be more womanly and understanding towards her mother. Lena is causing some slight anxiety just now. She is no doubt working under a change in her body, Menstruation! She flings herself about, lets things drop and acts rather like someone a little silly. Mabel is just a little tomboy, she is in good health and is going to school and learning music at home with Lena. She was at the North Road Clinic for X-rays in May 1934. Doctors think that there is a link missing from her spine, though we have not had any news of result of X-rays taken in July 1934.*"

George's next update is in 1936, when he wrote: "*George started a stage career with a Mr .Hinge at the Empire Theatre, Gateshead on Tyne. First production entitled "Blaydon Races", seemingly this is for a 14 week contract with more productions to follow.*"

Sadly there are no entries between 1936 and 1942. During this time war broke out and their eldest son George, his final diary entries are below:

"SEPTEMBER 1942, *Edna passed away at Wingrove Hospital maternity ward on Wednesday August 26th 1942 after giving birth to a baby boy on Sunday August 23rd at 4pm. Haemorrhage was supposed cause. George Rankin and I were last to see her on 25th August at 8.15pm when she talked to us quite sensibly and rational. She was laid to rest in St. Andrews on Saturday August 29th 1942.*"

"SEPTEMBER 10TH 1942, *Letter from George in Italy.*"

***"SEPTEMBER 17TH 1942** Edna's little son went to Dr. Barnado's Home near Harrogate on Thursday September 17th 1942."*

"Post card from concentration camp in Italy, saying son George is prisoner in their hands. Captured in Libya. Sent airmail letter to him on Friday September 18th 1942 telling him of Edna's passing."

***"AUGUST 1944,** Went to Harrogate to see Edna's kiddie near his 2nd birthday. Looked tip top condition, very pleased to see the way he was looked after, Millie was with me."*

***"MAY 2ND 1947,** Daughter born to Lena named Linda at Chiswick Hospital, London"*

***"APRIL 27TH 1958,** Ernest Elder, younger brother died suddenly in Street in Croxley Green, when going to Church with his 12 year old girl. Interned at Watford on May 2nd 1958."*

George was my Great-Grandfather, and although he stopped writing in 1958, he and Millie continued to live in Northumbria until Millie passed away in 1972, aged 72 years. Soon after Millie had passed away George moved in with his youngest daughter Mabel and her family in Newcastle, later moving to Luton to live with his daughter Lena, my grandmother. He lived with Lena and her husband William until he passed away peacefully in his sleep on 9th November 1980 at the age of 88.

George and Mildred's three surviving children were **George, Lena and Mabel.**

George returned from Italy unharmed. He married Amy Tate on Christmas Day in 1939. Amy and George had three children, and eight grandchildren, his children were; Ann born in 1941, David born in 1946 and Jacqueline born in 1959. George lived out his life in Barclay Place in Newcastle and died on 13th June 1976.

Mabel worked at Robinsons printers in Newcastle prior to marrying George Cresswell on April 6th 1946. She continued to work after her marriage as a cashier at The Royalty Cinema in Newcastle until it closed down. Mabel and George had a daughter Maureen born on 25th June 1948. They later separated in 1960. Mabel had two more children with her new partner Thomas Chaplehow, Stephen born on 19th June 1960 and Michael born on 8th October 1962. Mabel had two grandchildren, Gary born 1971, and Andrew born in 1976. Mabel passed away on 17th August 1993.

Lena worked in Armstrong ammunitions factory during the war and later spent most of her life in the Printing trade, she married William Joseph Arthur Winfield on 7th November 1923. Lena and William had two daughters Linda born on 2nd May 1947 and Vivienne born 11th September 1951. Lena and William moved away from Newcastle in 1962 as William transferred from The Northumbrian Police force to The British London Transport Police. They moved to Luton in Bedfordshire, where George later joined them. Their youngest daughter had three children, Darren born 1970, Richard born 1972, and Claire (myself) born 1976. Lena passed away on 19th September 1992 after suffering with dementia. William died within the year.

CLAIRE LOUISE THOMAS

Lightning Source UK Ltd.
Milton Keynes UK
UKOW050337191111

182324UK00002B/2/P